Dog Walks Man

A Six-Legged Odyssey

John Zeaman

Map illustrations by Claire Zeaman

LYONS PRESS
Guilford, Connecticut
An imprint of Globe Pequot Press

For Janet, Claire, and Alex

Lyons Press is an imprint of Globe Pequot Press.

Project editor: Gregory Hyman
Layout artist: Melissa Evarts
Text design: Sheryl P. Kober

Library of Congress Cataloging-in-Publication Data is available on file.

ISBN 978-1-59921-963-9

Printed in the United States of America

10 9 8 7 6 5 4 3 2 1

THE CREEK

RIDING STABLES

FOXES

CONTENTS

Contents

INTRODUCTION

When I first had the idea for this book, I mentioned it to a book-editor friend at a party.

"What's there to tell?" she asked, eyebrows raised. "What's there to know about walking a dog?"

In fact, the idea wasn't all that clear in my mind, so I did a lot of reflecting—while walking the dog, naturally—as to whether the everyday experiences and thoughts that I was having could be of interest to anyone.

Perhaps a more adventurous angle was needed, I thought. I recalled John Steinbeck's *Travels with Charley,* in which the author described his experiences driving cross-country with his standard poodle—the same breed of dog that I have had.

Why not do something like that, I thought. My dog, Pete, and I could cross America, too. Except we would walk. What had Thoreau said? "If you are ready to leave father and mother, and brother and sister, and wife and child and friends, and never see them again—if you have paid your debts, and made your will, and settled all your affairs, and are a free man—then you are ready for a walk."

But I was far from meeting Thoreau's requirements for taking the big walk. Hadn't paid my debts, had no will, hadn't settled any affairs, and was in no way "free." I had two children, a mortgage, and I needed every penny of my salary as a newspaper art critic.

Besides, walking across America, dog or no dog, sounded pretty daunting. Steinbeck, I noticed in rereading his book, was in his fifties—about my age—when he took his trip. Despite a custom-made truck and its well-stocked camper-cabin, he still fretted and worried for a month before finding the courage to go.

I began to recall cross-country hitchhiking trips I had made as a college student, and the mostly dreary, godforsaken places I had found myself in. At nineteen, there had at least been some romance to the experience—and the prospect of a ride. This time around, I'd be a middle-aged man walking his dog along some strip of highway outside Wichita Falls, Texas, or Billings, Montana.

I had to face it. I wasn't an adventurer.

So this book is an anti-adventure story.

My book-editor acquaintance was right. There is nothing to know, in the conventional sense, about walking the dog. There are few outdoor activities less athletic, strenuous, or dangerous. There really is no technique involved. You can't look back over years of it and take satisfaction in the progress you've made. There's no dog walker's high that comes after the third trip around the block.

So how does this seemingly mundane chore end up at the center of a person's life?

Good question.

It reminds me of something that my son, Alex, did when he was three. My wife, Janet, and I had taken our two children to the origami Christmas tree workshop at the Museum of Natural History. Japanese ladies were folding colored paper into ornamental shapes, some classic, some seasonally appropriate: cranes, doves, reindeer, sleighs, Santas, and so on. One of the volunteers handed one to my son. It was a dog. He studied the small elegant form in his hand and began to unfold it. The art critic in me wanted to reach out and stop him—someone had *made* this intricate little thing—but instead I watched as he carefully undid its complicated folds, revealing an abstract, accordion-like shape that he, in his innocence, found much more interesting than the folded form.

That was how it happened with me. Somewhere along the line, the simple flat form of a dog and a man walking along together began to unfold and reveal itself. A Buddhist might say—in that irritatingly complacent way Buddhists sometimes have—that the experience was always complete and perfect from the very beginning. But for me, a Western-style thinker, one thing follows another through time—just like a man and his dog on a walk.

People and dogs have been hanging around together for a long time. Scientists keep moving the date of the association further and further back in time. Currently the relationship is said to be more than 100,000 years old. That's older than the written language, older than the wheel, older than farming, older than art. At some point—and no one can say quite when—dogs and humans formed a genuine partnership. That partnership invariably involved going out in the world together—whether to hunt, to herd, to patrol borders, to fight, to go after varmints, or to move sleds.

Most dogs today no longer have any serious jobs. Nor do most people have the sorts of jobs in which dogs can be of assistance.

What remains is the walk.

So, the dog walk, I like to think, has a deep and resonant echo. It's a connection with our more primitive past. When my dog tugs me out the door, down the steps, and into the world, he pulls me out of myself, out of my complicated human life of news, bills, work, responsibilities, and ceaseless chatter—and into a much simpler existence, one that animal psychologist Konrad Lorenz once called "animal nirvana . . . an unequalled panacea for mental strain, true balm for the mind of hurried, worried, modern man, which has been rubbed sore in so many places."

Not the least of my dog's services is that he gives me no choice. There are days when I don't work, days when I may not have a regular meal, days when I barely talk to another person. In a pinch, I've skipped brushing my teeth, forgotten to comb my hair. But it's very hard, almost impossible, to skip walking the dog (unless you can pass the job off to someone else).

Even during a marital rupture, when I lived apart from my wife . . . even then, I would drive over from my miserable bachelor apartment on the wrong side of town and take Pete for his walk. My role as husband and father could be altered and renegotiated, but not my responsibility to the dog.

The things we can't get out of often have unexpected value. And, as the years have gone by, I've noticed a strange phenomenon. More and more of my life has become bound up with this simple activity. Exercise? I get it walking the dog. Contemplation? I get some of my best thinking done. Human companionship? I've made a great friend. Adventure? Every dog walk is different. A sense of eternity? Every dog walk is the same.

Technology still hasn't found a way to modernize dog walking. Despite expandable leashes, flashing collars, and doggy raincoats, it's still fundamentally this ancient, simple activity: a person tending to his domesticated animal. This application of feet to dirt and the slower pace makes dog walkers more observant than most people. You and the dog do a lot of reconnoitering. You tend to retrace your steps. You form attachments to places—even small insignificant places—just as Thoreau did to Walden Pond.

Sometimes dog walking seemed a return to a boyhood world I'd forgotten. I found myself in places like woods, abandoned lots, railroad right-of-ways—those fringe places of which there seem to be fewer and fewer nowadays. I rediscovered the aimlessness of childhood wandering, and came upon dams, and huts, and forts like those I'd left behind more than forty years ago.

There is a hope that a dog injects into every walk, more than a hope—an expectation, really—that this is going to be something wonderful. You'll see, says the dog, something great is going to happen—just you wait.

CHAPTER ONE

Duped

Some dads don't know what hit them. The beagle-dad went by our house today. He's new to the neighborhood, a young father who walks the family dog before he dresses for work. He shuffles along in baggy jeans and an old work shirt, his hair sticking up every which way. In contrast, the dog always looks fresh, bright-eyed, sleek—not a hair out of place.

There's something comical in the tethered condition of these two. The dog takes long, thoughtful pauses at the bases of trees before anointing each spot with a few drops of urine. The man's attention flits desperately from one thing to another: the trees, the clouds, the facades of houses, the conditions of people's lawns. He seems to find it all unsatisfying, unworthy of his attention. He gives a tug on the leash. The dog lifts its leg again and gives one more squirt for good measure.

He is a member of the fraternity of dog-walker fathers, or, in my secret parlance, the brotherhood of dupes. He doesn't know it yet or understand why it's the natural order of things and nothing to worry about. I wish I could help him over the hump, but this is one of those things a man needs to find out for himself.

His family profile is the same as ours. They moved here from the city. They partook of the pleasures of a big house and backyard, and a basketball hoop in the driveway. Then, against all reason, they gambled on another notch of happiness and got a dog.

Why do people do this? Why do parents with young children—despite having more responsibilities and pressures than ever before—take on the additional burden of a dog? You don't have to invest in those *Lassie* stories about dogs disarming burglars or dragging people from burning rooms. Young families get a dog because dogs are less prone to self-consciousness and doubt than people are. People are dreamier and more restless. They are given to wondering how life might be different here or there, perhaps with an entirely different set of people.

Dogs share none of this. They know they are in the right place. They bring to the human family a powerful animal certainty, one borne of instinct and the cohesiveness of the pack. They are family glue.

Ours was a family of four, recently transplanted from Manhattan to a New Jersey suburb. We had traded in a semi-bohemian life for a house in a safe neighborhood and a full-time job for me. Formerly a freelance writer and a painter, I had taken a job on a large suburban daily newspaper as an art critic. It was an abrupt change. One day we were living in a former zipper factory where the heat went off at 6:00 p.m., the trash had to be secretly dumped in street receptacles, and the car was in constant danger of being towed away. The next day we had a thermostat, trash pickup at the side of the house, and our own garage.

Our town was perched on the back slope of the Palisades, its proximity to the city seemingly a trick of space and time. After crossing the George Washington Bridge, we were whisked through a mad thirty-second tangle of loops, overpasses, and branching highways before sliding down an exit ramp and finding ourselves beneath a cool arboreal canopy while negotiating narrow, angular streets.

Moving day was like the tornado sequence in *The Wizard of Oz*. We were lifted out of the stark black-and-white drama of Manhattan and deposited with a great whoosh in a place that was as gaudily colored as the land of the munchkins: yellow daffodils, candy-colored azaleas, and purple rhododendrons with crickets and tree frogs thrumming our welcome.

Spring in the suburbs.

Claire was four when we moved, Alex just one. It was a sweet time of life. Love flowed in every direction, hitting all its intended targets. Well, there was one small exception. Claire, like many little girls, yearned for something to nurture. She wanted a pet.

So began her zookeeper phase. We became major patrons of the local pet store. We started out with goldfish. Soon we graduated to lizards. Then turtles. And then finches. Then a parakeet. Then gerbils. The more the merrier. We acquired glass tanks, cages, aerators, gravel, bags of cedar shavings, electrically heated "rocks," feeding bowls, water bottles, little nets, plastic tubes, exercise wheels. We even adopted animals from the wild—a small snake, a baby squirrel.

Claire gave all her pets dignified, human names. Not Zippy or Fudge, but Daphne, Jason, Lillian, Robert—like characters out of *Upstairs, Downstairs*. But their lives were anything but dignified. The zebra finches, Louis and Victoria, nudged their eggs out of the nest and smashed them at the bottom of the cage. The lizards required the sacrifice of live crickets. Even the innocent-looking gerbils, which stood on their haunches like miniature kangaroos, routinely practiced incest, infanticide, and patricide. Males tried to mate with females while they were giving birth. A father might eat a baby or two. Sons grew up and tried to kill their fathers.

The hoped-for nurturing experiences had turned into grim lessons in disease and death. The tragic nadir came when the gregarious parakeet, Charlie, who was free to fly around Claire's room, somehow climbed down into the gerbil tank and was brutally attacked by George and Sophia and their son, Scott. He died on the veterinarian's operating table.

Soon, a corner of our backyard was dotted with tiny graves. Their stones bore dates, names, and tributes written in black laundry pen. ("Alan/ A carefree young gerbil/ Oct. 7, 1986–Nov. 30, 1986.") Raccoons and possums dug up the graves, discarded the cardboard coffins and tissue-paper liners, and made off with the corpses. The children's mourning gave way to morbid fascination, and soon they were bringing over curious friends to see the desecrated graves.

But Charley's death had been traumatic for all of us. We had had enough with the short and brutish lives of small, caged animals.

Looking back, our path mimicked the stages of evolution. We had moved up the phylogenetic scale until we reached an animal that, in size and intelligence, lived closer to the human plane. It was time to get a dog.

How did we end up with a standard poodle? Pure chance. I met a man with a poodle at the town's Arbor Day festivities. This dog seemed remarkably self-possessed. In the midst of much confusion—kids wielding squirt guns, skateboards zooming by—he sat alert and curious but unperturbed. Like a person in a dog suit, I thought.

Poodles, I later discovered, are retrievers. And like all retrievers (who must learn to fetch downed waterfowl without succumbing to the temptation to rip them to pieces), they are bred to be calm and reasonable. I also learned that the eccentric poodle clip has practical origins. Trainers shaved poodles' hindquarters so the dogs could swim faster. Puffballs insulated the joints against cold water. As in art, innovation gave way to mannerism, resulting in that affected topiary look.

But who said a poodle had to look like that? Couldn't one have a scruffy poodle?

Janet pointed out that there would still be the expense of haircuts, fancy or otherwise.

"We could get clippers, do it ourselves," I said.

She looked at me skeptically.

Getting a dog is like having a baby: You remember every step along the way. Soon we were driving up the Merritt Parkway to see a lady who had some poodle pups. My mother, visiting for the weekend, sat in the backseat with the squirming children and took the role of skeptic. "This is so sudden," she said. "How do you know this is a reputable breeder?"

My mother, former owner of a very neurotic Welsh terrier, believed that the purchase of a dog should be preceded by months of research and negotiations culminating in a long-distance trip. She had driven all the way to West Virginia for her terrier. She thought we were acting impulsively.

The breeder, a suburban mother in jeans and work shirt, led us out to the backyard, where several puppies were wandering about. They were all black and bigger than I had imagined they would be. I had pictured a dog that would fit into a shoe box, like a Christmas present. But these puppies were already about the size of cocker spaniels.

There was a child's plastic pushcart in the yard, and Alex soon had one of them in it and was wheeling the puppy around. My mother kibitzed with loud stage whispers.

"Don't take that one," she said. "Too passive."

Seeing that we were undecided, the breeder produced another dog from the house. She had set him aside for someone, but they hadn't made a deposit. Perhaps it was only the enthusiasm of being reunited with his littermates, but this pup put on a lively show. He was so happy and spirited, running circles around all the others, that he seemed like the clear winner.

"Let's get this one," said Claire. Alex seconded the motion.

"Get a female," my mother said. "They're more family oriented. Better with children."

I shrugged, recalling the male poodle from the Arbor Day celebration.

"Don't rush into this," my mother whispered. "Wait until you find the right dog."

Janet picked him up and nuzzled with him. "He's so soft," she said.

He chased the children around the yard. One by one, we fell in love with him.

A half hour later, after buying several hundred more dollars' worth of accessories, including a metal training crate that the breeder swore by, we were on our way home with our new dog.

Stretched out across the three laps in the backseat, he threw up repeatedly on the hour-long trip.

A mere exchange of money, and a life was ours. What did this puppy know about us? We had taken him from his home, separated him from his mother and his littermates, put him in this strange nausea-inducing conveyance, and yet he couldn't have been more trusting.

At home, the kids gave him a tour of the house. He stuck his head in Alex's closet and emerged with a sneaker in his mouth. He scrambled under Claire's bed and pulled out a dust-covered tennis ball. Everything he did was an event: his first drink of water, his first dog biscuit, his first pee in the backyard—and his second on the dining room rug.

The children, given the job of naming him, deliberated on the back steps. The puppy sat staring back at them, a black shape against the bright green grass. Various names were bandied about. Had things gone differently, Pete might have been a Willie, or even a Willard (Claire's penchant for formal names).

At one point, Alex wanted to name him Egon, after a character in *Ghostbusters,* his favorite movie.

This was soundly ridiculed by Claire, but Alex, slow to give up on the idea of a Ghostbuster dog, suggested naming the dog after another of the characters.

"How about Peter Venkman?" he said.

The puppy, following the flight of a squawking mockingbird overhead, lost his balance and flopped over, showing a plump pink belly.

"Another Ghostbuster?" said Claire. "That is *so stupid.*"

"Don't say stupid. You're *stupid,*" said Alex. His large blue eyes teared up a little.

"Dogs don't have first names and last names," said Claire. "Anyway, if he had a last name, it would be our last name, not *Venkman.*"

"Okay," said Alex. "Peter. Let's call him Peter."

Claire didn't say anything.

"Come on, Claire," said Alex.

"I'm thinking," said Claire. She tried it out. "Peter," she called to the puppy. "Hey, Peter. Hi Pete. Come here, Petey."

The puppy, who had been lying on his side, perked up his ears, vaulted to his feet, and, not surprisingly, trotted right over to us.

And that was that. By an improbable association with a crackpot movie character played by Bill Murray, our dog ended up with one of the most common of all dog names.

Then there was the business of the crate. Crates were new to me. I never remember anyone having such a thing when I was a kid. But I had let the breeder talk me into buying one, and now I had to assemble it and explain its purpose to the children.

"The crate is like the dog's den," I said, quoting from the booklet that came with it. "A dog won't go to the bathroom in its den, because that's where it has to lie down."

I was having trouble getting the sides of the thing to stand up. I almost had the top affixed when the whole thing crashed down like a pile of cymbals. The puppy retreated to a corner.

After much struggling, I finally had it all together, upright and intact. I put on the door.

"There," I said.

We stepped back to take a look.

"It looks like a cage," said Alex.

"Well . . ." I started to say.

"You said *a den*," said Alex.

Of course he was right. It was a cage. It was silly to say otherwise. But I had paid for this thing, and there was the matter of housebreaking the dog, so I got out the pamphlet—"Creating a Canine Haven"—and reviewed some of its principal points with the children.

"The dog feels safe and secure in the crate," I read.

"Why can't our house be his den?" Alex asked.

"Real dog dens are small," I explained. "The human house seems much too big to be a den, so they treat the attic or the basement like the outdoors and think it's okay to pee there."

"Let's see how he likes it," said Claire.

She picked him up and put him in and I closed the door. We all drew in close to watch. Pete moved about uneasily, turning one way and then the other. Then he began to whimper.

"He doesn't like it!" said Alex.

"He'll get used to it," I said.

"Look at his eyes," said Claire. "They look so sad."

Pete, as it turned out, never got used to the crate. We tried. We really did. Every time we put him in it, he made a fuss. We tried all the suggestions in the pamphlet, including shaking a can of pennies to discourage whining. But in truth, Petey's vocal protests were the least of it. We could have put up with that.

It was, as Claire said, *those eyes.*

He looked like a political prisoner.

Someone once asked the solitary poet Rainer Maria Rilke why he didn't get a dog to keep him company. Rilke, the hypersensitive romantic, answered that dogs had half-human souls and were he to live with one, he would not be able to resist breaking off pieces of his heart like "bits of dog biscuit" for the dog.

That pretty much summed up our situation. We were too sensitive and our dog was too human. When you petted him on the head, he gulped with emotion.

So Pete came out of the crate, and the crate went up in the attic.

There were some consequences. He got into Janet's closet and chewed up her delicate Italian shoes. Once, locked in the basement while we were out, he clawed a hole through the thin plywood on one side of the hollow-core door.

But he paid back our softheartedness. Within two weeks he'd housebroken himself.

In the beginning, of course, everyone in our family was happy to share the dog-walking responsibility. I remember standing at the window with Janet in one of those moist-eyed Hallmark moments, watching our two children walking up the hill, Claire holding the loop of the leash and Alex with a mostly symbolic grip on the leash's middle.

Those moments were few and far between.

"Petey pulls too hard," one of them would say. Or *"Petey chased a squirrel and I scraped my knee,"* or *"Petey pooped on the neighbor's lawn and I think they were looking out the window."*

Thus, the period of egalitarian sharing of dog-walking duties came to an end. After a mere six months, they had all weaned themselves from the task. *This is nature's way,* Pete's consoling eyes seemed to say. We were partners. I had become our family's dog-walking dupe.

Everyone accepted this as the natural order of things. It made life much simpler for everyone, including Pete. Now, when he wanted to go out, he no longer had to wander from one pack member to another with beseeching looks. He could focus exclusively on me.

I complained a little, but I convinced myself that the job had fallen to me as the man of the family. I tried to initiate new routines that I thought would reflect the masculine nature of our relationship—one characterized by few words and tacit under-standings. I didn't say, "Come on, Pete," as the others had done, when it was time for a walk. I whistled to him, a short, sharp whis-tle, like the Lone Ranger used with his horse. Pete would barrel into the room, skidding to a stop in front of me. Then he'd sit on his haunches, tail thumping, while I clipped on the leash. I could feel him vibrating with anticipation.

I'd pat his flank and murmur, "Good dog." When the metal clip snapped, he turned into a dervish. I'd yank open the front door and we'd go bouncing down the steps, the world tilting this way and that like the handheld camera in a scene from *Cops!*

Soon I was bonding with other dog-walking dupes.

Everyone said the same thing. *"Kids wanted a dog..." "We talked it over..." "They promised they'd walk it..."*

Knowing nods.

My favorite was Richard, who lived around the corner. His daughter, Sara, a classmate of Claire's, had begged for a dog. Unfor-tunately, she was allergic. But Richard and his wife—enlightened, problem-solving parents—had researched the issue and discov-ered a breed, the African Basenji, that didn't shed.

Soon they had purchased one from a breeder. The dog was medium size, sleek, and angular, with a pointy face, curled tail, and longish legs. In addition to not shedding, she didn't bark. Her breed was strangely silent, excitable but not vocal.

They named her Jambo, the Swahili word for hello.

Richard was sweet and bearish, with a full beard and a mouth full of oversized teeth. He had no interest in dog walking. He wasn't the walking type. He was the stand-around-and-schmooze type. I'd encounter him about a half-block from his house, feet anchored to the ground, playing out Jambo on an expandable leash. Protruding from his back pocket would be the blue plastic wrapper from the *New York Times*—the poop bag of choice for well-informed suburbanites.

Jambo would run circles around Richard and Richard would have to keep switching the leash from hand to hand to keep from getting tangled. He looked like a cowboy doing an elaborate lasso trick.

What I liked the best about Richard was that we shared an understanding of our duped conditions. He'd smile sheepishly at me and I'd smile back the same way. Our smiles said: *"Here we are again, out with our dogs, waiting for them to poop so that we can pick it up. Could anything be more ridiculous?"*

But these same smiles communicated a deeper self-awareness. We were out here because, in becoming fathers, we had changed from self-centered young men to self-sacrificing parents. *We know we are being taken advantage of and yet, for the first time in our lives, we don't really mind . . .*

Chapter Two

Gratitude

The stage was set, all the characters in place: the happy family, their sensitive and loyal canine companion, and this seemingly minor issue resolved of who would walk him. In most stories, the narrator would move on to other developments in this family's life: the growth of the children, the course of a marriage and careers, and the various crises, triumphs, and defeats that every family experiences.

This narrative follows a different trajectory. The other characters recede a bit, and the reader is invited to follow the narrator out the door and . . .

Where? Where does he go?

Where does any dog walker go? Around the block, down the boulevard, over to the park, into the woods, out to the quarry, across the lot, along the railroad tracks, down the grassy strip, into the alley, or out to the old ball field.

Put another way, you go out. And then you come back. It's simple, but not so simple. In the middle, things happen.

Am I making too much of this?

Well, that's the dog's fault, you see.

A dogless person can minimize the significance of such departures and returns. The dogless person puts on a hat, announces, "I'm going out," and barely makes a ripple in the firmament. It's different with a dog. The dog need only hear the word "out" to understand that something momentous is about to happen. It celebrates ecstatically. It leaps, it shimmies, it turns in deliriously happy circles.

The same on coming back. A dog catching sight of home at the end of a walk can raise the level of emotion to that of Odysseus catching sight of Ithaca on the horizon.

In the beginning, I walked around the block. Or a couple of blocks. It didn't seem to matter. That it didn't matter was in itself novel. It had been a long time since I had gone out without any particular destination or direction, without knowing whether I was going to turn left or turn right at the end of the front walk.

I had no idea where all this was leading, though I like to think that even then I felt something tugging below the surface, the way a fisherman feels vibrations on a taut line and wonders whether something's biting or it's just the weight brushing the bottom.

The simple aimlessness of it made me feel like a kid again. Back then, I was always out, had to be out, couldn't bear not being out. Home from school, I shed books and disappeared, the parental refrain of "be home in time for dinner" trailing behind me. After dinner, I agitated for release again and was, if lucky, granted an extension, "until the streetlights come on." Saturdays, I would be AWOL from breakfast till dinnertime. My rule was simple. Out was better than in. Even if there was no one to play with, I could sit on the curb and practice my spitting, or throw rocks left-handed, or watch ants consume a melted Popsicle. Anything other than being under a parent's watchful eye. Indoors was predictable and safe. Outdoors, things happened. Or, at least they could.

Pete, with his boundless enthusiasm for the outside world, was like the reincarnation of that juvenile self. We'd hit the sidewalk and, like two kids with nothing special to do, spend a half hour meandering about. We were suburban vagabonds. In the mornings, with the whole world rushing to get somewhere, there was something almost subversive about roaming around with a companion who had no responsibilities.

We walked the irregular streets of our hilly town. We each had our compulsions. I revived the childhood aversion to stepping on cracks. Pete made sure that every tree was marked with his scent.

Even the treks through bad weather reminded me of childhood. Oh, I'd grumble about it, but secretly, I liked having an excuse to stomp around in the snow or the driving rain.

At night, Pete and I would escape the sometimes-suffocating sweetness of family life—the pajamas and stories, the smell of toothpaste and sheets, the damp goodnight kisses and prolonged hugs. We'd slip out into the silky night like a pair of teenage boys with high hopes for a Saturday night. We'd walk beneath the streetlights from one pool of light to the next. The people in the houses would drift past the windows like aquarium fish. Pete, with his black coat, was practically invisible in the dark stretches, and I would let him off the leash.

There were a surprising number of animals out and about on these jaunts. We encountered possums, some as large as small dogs. They had red-rimmed eyes, hairless pink tails, and walked with an awkward gait, moving the legs on the same side of the body together, rather than alternately as most four-legged animals do. When Pete confronted one, it would freeze guiltily, as if horrified just to be seen. I never saw one play dead, but they never ran away either, much to Pete's disappointment. The raccoons, by comparison, were charming rogues who knew how to handle themselves. They were all around us, scrambling down from the trees, boldly ransacking garbage cans, scuttling humpbacked across streets, and ducking into storm sewers, their own subterranean transportation system. Sometimes, after such a retreat, you'd see one peering back through the slotted opening, looking like an imprisoned burglar.

Night also taught me the therapeutic benefits of dog walking. In those days, I was writing a lot about the news of art—auctions, art thefts, art vandalism, museum expansions, museum politics, gallery scandals, censorship controversies. The reporting was hard work and frequently kept me late at the office. When I got home, Pete was often the only one still up. He'd greet me with an exuberant tap dance, clearly hoping for a walk. Maybe I'd feel a little put upon at first—I'd worked hard, I was tired, I needed a drink . . .

But the night was soothing. I could clear my head of whatever controversy or auction spectacle I'd been wrapped up in. And there were better things to pay attention to. Who cared why the Japanese were paying millions for van Goghs and Renoirs when the trees above my head were chirping with invisible life? Were there really tiny frogs up there? What were the Culture Wars compared to the mystery of the Harvest Moon, as big as a paper lantern at the horizon, as small as a quarter at the zenith?

And every once in a while, there'd be a night where the simple act of going away from the house and coming back was like a scene from *It's a Wonderful Life*.

I remember one snowy night. This was one of those times when I really didn't want to go out with the dog. There had been a party, I was a little tipsy, the house was warm, my bed beckoned. I had practically forgotten that we *had* a dog until I heard his desperate reminder, a single yip, issued from the direction of the front door.

I felt put upon. What was the story with this *animal*, this beast with its primitive needs? How could it continually rely on me to provide this escort service? Was it my fault that dogs hadn't kept up with their evolutionary development? Where did this sense of entitlement come from? Was there a clause in some ancient contract between people and dogs?

I tried the last refuge of the reluctant dog walker—opening the back door and pointing to the backyard. Shouldn't that be good enough? Do I expect a trip to the bathroom to be recreational? Get it over with, while I watch from the window. But Pete was having none of it. It was a showdown. All or nothing. He was incredibly stubborn sometimes. It had to be a real walk, he and I together, out the front door into the bigger world.

Finally, cursing loudly, I surrendered. Pete watched my every move as I put on boots, coat, scarf, and hat. At least he had the tact to forego the celebratory tap dance.

Out we went into the not-at-all-gentle night.

The snow was coming down hard, in big, sticky flakes. I shuffled down the walk, plowing two clean lines with my feet. The snow clung to every horizontal surface—tree branches, the curving contours of cars, house roofs, and porch railings.

The houses were all dark—not even the flicker of TV light. My virtuous neighbors were all asleep. No cars had come up the street yet. By morning, it would be plowed, shoveled, compressed, salted, melted, blown away. But for now, snowflakes lay undisturbed in airy piles.

I let Pete off the leash. He trotted ahead, up the hill, pausing to raise his leg at the fire hydrant. Even the hydrant's small hexagonal top had a perfect plug of snow standing on it. The air was bracing, like a pinch of snuff in each nostril.

It was, in a word, beautiful. And I found myself reflecting once again on this minor miracle of dog walking: how, forced to do something—even something that you really, really didn't want to do—you could end up feeling *grateful* for it.

I felt wide-awake and strangely energetic. In the streetlights, I could see the precise slant of the snowfall. The low cloud ceiling reflected the light from the nearby city, making the sky unnaturally bright. I made a few snowballs and tossed them in Pete's direction. They disintegrated in the snow at his feet. Finally, he caught one on a fly—or at least half of it.

We came around the last leg of our around-the-block journey. The house came into view. Its simple rectangular shape, its snow-covered roof and smoking chimney made it look like a child's drawing. Curtains framed the darkened windows of the rooms. Up there, on the second floor, the children and Janet were sleeping.

How had all this happened? Out of a series of unplanned moves—marrying, having children, moving here—life had taken a good turn. It had all added up to something, after all.

Pete peed on his favorite telephone pole, the last stop before the house. Claire's cat, who had slipped out with us, was pacing in front of the door. I loved the animals' sense of entitlement, their certainty that this place belonged to them, as well as to us. I had created not just a home—but a den, too! I let them both in ahead of me.

Soon we'd all be asleep. Pete would find a spot on the floor of the upstairs landing, or, more likely, on one of the children's beds. He'd lose himself in dreams, feet twitching in anticipation of tomorrow's adventures. He'd be the first one up, nudging the oblivious children awake.

There was no sleeping in when fresh snow was on the ground.

✤

CHAPTER THREE
Safety and Adventure

An artist friend from Manhattan came over to visit one day. He took one look around the neighborhood and said, "You've moved into one of your own paintings."

I saw what he meant. The paintings he was referring to, done when we lived in the city, had been partly inspired by medieval illuminations. There had been a book I liked at the time, a facsimile of a Catholic prayer book, a *Book of Hours,* made for a French duke. I kept noticing how often the people in the book were depicted in protected spaces. They were inside the walls of monasteries, fortified towns, or castles. Outside was the scary wild—dark forests in which wolves and bears and highwaymen lurked. Inside, there was music and religion and pageantry.

What the paintings said to me was: *It's dangerous out there, but in here it is safe.* In retrospect, the appeal was probably rooted in our own living circumstances. We had begun to feel under siege. We had two children by this time, and some of the charm of living in a former zipper factory had begun to wear thin. A resurgence of commercial activity in our once moribund Garment District neighborhood had brought noise, crime, and a new and hostile landlord. Garbage trucks whined and roared throughout the night, waking and frightening the children. Holdup artists arrived, attracted by stories of immigrant businessmen with pockets of cash. They worked the small elevators, using the elevator's cover to rob everybody before sending the victims up and making their escape.

If, on some days we didn't have to worry about muggers on the elevator, it was only because the elevator was out of service. Janet and I would hoof the five flights up the dirty back stairs, often climbing over sleeping homeless men. One day, coming out of our building while pushing Claire in a stroller, we found ourselves in the middle of a street arrest. A huge detective's pistol was hoisted in the air. I turned toward Janet, or where Janet had been the second before, and saw her halfway up the block with the stroller.

So I created my own modern interpretation of medieval sanctuaries. I painted things in a flat, symbolist style, reducing everything to cutout shapes—like paper dolls or Egyptian art. I mixed in a little urban architecture and some menacing garbage trucks, while inside my enclosure a medieval man and woman tended to sheep, rocked the baby, grew flowers, and played the lute. Behind them, a flock of doves rose like musical notes.

My artist friend had a point. Our neighborhood, which sat on a steep, terraced hill, did have some of that storybook quality that had gone into my pictures: the steeply pitched roofs poking up through the foliage, the carefully tended yards with their stepping-stone walkways, the mounds of colorful impatiens at the bases of trees. It was telling a story that was similar to that of my paintings and the medieval paintings: *here, it is safe.*

We had chosen this particular community both because of its proximity to the city and because it had a reputation for being an interesting town. What specifically caught my eye in the real estate brochure was the phrase, "artist colony." At the time, I don't think I really knew what "artist colony" meant, but it evoked an attractive image of barefoot artists living in bungalows.

For a while, that was probably how it was. In the late nineteenth century, Manhattan artists crossed the Hudson in search of more space and a cheaper cost of living. At the time, communities like mine had plenty of empty sheds or barns that could be had for next to nothing. Artists could do a combination of the Impressionist thing and the Thoreau thing. Soon a few "colonies" sprouted up. Many artists passed through or had sojourns in this area. Typical of these was surrealist Man Ray, who, in the years before World War I, painted Cézannesque landscapes before decamping for Paris.

But cycles of gentrification had already begun. A clever New York advertising man came up with the line, "Athens of The East," to lure professors from Columbia University. By the turn of the century, the town was already a suburb. Artists still came, but they weren't going barefoot anymore. They were more respectable types, family men with jobs. Some taught at the Art Students League or the National Academy of Design. Others were artist-illustrators for magazines like *The Saturday Evening Post* or *House and Garden*. Pictures in the town library show students painting in the Meadowlands, shading themselves with parasols and straw hats.

Janet and I fit the established migration pattern perfectly. Artist colony or no artist colony, we were ready to belong. Perhaps it was our parental genes kicking in, but after the anonymity of a big city, we yearned for small-town familiarity. We wanted to go to open-school nights and Christmas concerts, to shake hands with the mayor, to vote for the school budget, to be on a first-name basis with the druggist and the hardware-store guy. We wanted to watch our kids sled down our street. We wanted the whole apple pie.

If you want to know a place, get a dog and walk it. The dog's curiosity and alertness are contagious. You stop a lot. You look. You learn. I looked at other people's houses with the enhanced curiosity of a new homeowner. I admired broad porches, jaunty turrets, and fanlight entryways. There was, I began to realize, an element of masquerade in house design. Houses donned mansard roofs to look French, orange tiles to look Mediterranean, and a little dark timbering for that Bavarian or Tudor look. I saw how they grew, sprouting wings, dormers, and greenhouse additions, as if they could never be big enough.

Sometimes, I'd have a glance into a scholar's book-lined study or see one of those Palladian windows that the artist houses had, and I'd yearn a little for the town's Golden Age when Nobel Prize winners walked the sidewalks, well-known artists painted murals in the schools, and soon-to-be-famous actors starred in the community theater.

Then I fell in love with trees. Manhattan had trees, of course, but the canyons they grew in made them seem like potted plants. In the suburbs, trees were benevolent giants. They spread their leafy green crowns high to shade the streets and houses. While

Pete sniffed and anointed the roots, I studied their branching tops. I learned to recognize straight-trunked pin oaks, dense Norway maple, ungainly London plane, and the flowering Bradford pear. I even admired the lawns, symbol of all that was supposed to be sterile and controlling about the suburbs. I didn't believe in pouring all those fertilizers, pesticides, and herbicides into the ground, but wasn't the result, those soft green expanses, seductive?

It wasn't an accident that the early park-like suburbs evoked feelings of shelter and sanctuary. In fact, it was an instance of life imitating art. Commuters back then were supposed to return from the city, via ferry and train, to a place where rustic houses were arranged along streets that looked like quaint country lanes.

Everyone knew what this charming, restful village was supposed to look like because artists from Rembrandt to Boucher to van Gogh had been burnishing this imagery for hundreds of years: the thatched roof cottage beneath the spreading elms, the stately manor at the top of the hill. Designers such as Andrew Jackson Downing codified it into real houses and real landscapes and it came trickling down in illustrations, needlepoint, and house-pattern books as the ideal of *Home Sweet Home.*

Once you saw the intention, it was easy to see where the rest came from, how the sheltering trees contributed to the symbolism of comfort and retreat, and how the lawn functioned as a miniature meadow around each house, an apron of safety (lest the beasts from the forest get too close).

The reason we seemed to be living in a picture was because we sort of were. And Pete and I were part of it. We, too, were picturesque. Neighbors smiled at us when we went by. Who was more guileless, more benign? In the hierarchy of trustworthiness, we ranked right beneath mothers pushing baby carriages, fathers and sons playing catch, little girls dressed for church.

Of course, all this could get a bit too saccharine, even for someone like me, prone to having *It's a Wonderful Life* epiphanies on snowy nights. Safety can be oppressive. No sooner are you safe than you long for the wild. Even Thoreau, seemingly at home at Walden Pond, felt the need for a more rugged summer vacation in the much wilder Maine Woods and on the savage slopes of Mount Katahdin.

And that oppressiveness of safety, I suppose, is what propelled me up the hill that day. Pete and I started out on a regular walk and just kept going. We walked all the way up to the Palisades, out onto the George Washington Bridge, and across the river.

I don't know what got into me. It wasn't that far, but to get up on the bridge, we had to cross over highway overpasses and ascend a remote cage-enclosed stairway that went up the forested crest of the Palisades. From there a catwalk took us over some highway lanes and finally onto the pedestrian walkway leading to Manhattan. I don't like heights. Pete, it turned out—I could tell by his trembling legs—had his own canine acrophobia: fear of transparent grids with cars driving beneath them. He was better when we reached the solid-floored pedestrian walkway of the bridge, but I—gazing over the railing to the dizzying 300-foot drop that regularly beckoned to the suicidal—was worse.

We weren't cut out for this sort of thing, either of us, but one thing I learned: Even when a walk goes bad, a dog will stick it out with you. Pete and I against the bridge. We walked at double time. The bridge droned and vibrated incessantly.

Bicyclists pedaled by, helmeted heads down, rear ends up, obviously untroubled by stories of people who went over the rail. It took us a good half hour to get across. When we arrived, we were on the streets of Washington Heights, a neighborhood I didn't know. Friends were all subway rides away, and Pete wouldn't pass for a seeing-eye dog. Anyway, I had work to do. So, we got back on the bridge and did the return lap. And never did it again.

Dog walking is a hopeful condition. It can be a magic portal— and would be for me—but not into the world we'd left behind in Manhattan, or its substitute, the world my town left behind in the 1920s. Of course, I sometimes missed the excitement and sheer sexiness of Manhattan, that sense of living on the edge that made you feel brave and committed. I missed the life before children, before life revolved around mortgages, pediatric visits, and news stories about the culture wars.

It's a tricky balancing act, finding that point between safety and danger where you can feel both secure and adventurous. I used to read books about fishing by people who had given up jobs and careers to show up every day at a trout stream. What made them do it? They realized, after years of fortifying the walls, of making life safe and secure, that they also needed what was on the other side.

CHAPTER FOUR

Picking It Up

Nothing bedevils us dog walkers so much as having to pick up the poop. It is at once the raison d'être of dog walking and its most ticklish problem. It tests our patience, our problem-solving abilities, our ethical standards, our thresholds of squeamishness, even our dexterity.

One day, stuck in traffic on West 86th Street in Manhattan, I watched a stylish young woman pick up after a cocker spaniel. The dog had squatted down on the sidewalk close to a crowded bus stop. Several people stared with obvious disapproval. The woman, undaunted, performed a series of deft maneuvers. A plastic baggie appeared on her hand. Reining the dog in and kneeling down in her heels and tight skirt, she gingerly picked it up. Standing and letting the loop of the leash slide down her forearm, she reversed the baggie, turning it into a small compact package. She sealed it with a spin and a plastic tie, let the leash slip back into her hand, and continued on her way. As the traffic jam loosened, she walked to a corner basket and dropped the baggie in.

What aplomb, I thought. A woman who would be horrified to know that a piece of lettuce was stuck between her teeth had just calmly picked up a handful of warm dog crap and carried it down a busy city sidewalk. This kind of thing is so commonplace that we forget how fundamentally odd, how far outside the traditional norms of social behavior it is. An eighteenth-century New Yorker would have an easier time believing in a future of skyscrapers and helicopters than in one in which well-dressed ladies would pick up dog droppings.

In those days of Old New York, not only dogs, but also pigs, goats, and horses defecated in the street. The gutter was like an open sewer. Even after sewers were installed under the streets and cars replaced horses, dogs continued to use the street. "Curb your Dog" defined the border between the acceptable and the unacceptable. It remained that way well past the middle of the twentieth century when, in response to the Clean Water Act and various other environmental reforms, cities and towns adopted the so-called pooper-scooper laws.

Today, in New York City, fines of up to $2,000 can be levied against violators. The signs that warn of such fines often depict a stick figure wielding a long-handled metal device known as a "pooper-scooper." Its graphic clarity has made it a universal symbol, despite the fact that in twenty years of dog walking, I have seen maybe four people using them.

Now, a confession: I don't always pick up. I know this raises character questions. My wife will be horrified that I am making such a public admission. She is the sort of person who will pick up after a dog in the wilderness. In fact, she once did this on a family hike through a forest preserve, a place thick with trees, underbrush, and even large boulders that animals could discretely retreat behind to do their business. I tried to point out that no one picked up after the raccoons, foxes, and deer. I also pointed out that this was a carry-out-your-trash park, which meant that, technically speaking, the little bag would have to come home in the car with us.

None of these rationalizations carries any weight with my wife and others like her. To them, the ethics are simple. You do the right thing, or you do the wrong thing.

My ethics are situational. I would never fail to pick up after my dog on the sidewalk, someone's lawn, or the grassy strip. But when it comes to vacant lots, wooded side yards, and thick beds of ivy or pachysandra, I have been known to be a little less than vigilant.

My moral decline began—like so many—in a back alley.

This alley, which makes a dead-end at our back fence, has rustic charm, a reminder of a more genteel era when cars were garaged at the rear of the house. Naturally, I found it a congenial place to walk the dog. Once in there, was it any surprise that my eyes were drawn to the tall weeds, the piles of leaves, the casual heaps of discarded branches? Or that, at night, I was pleased to find it deserted, silent, and surprisingly dark?

Wasn't this overgrown, often muddy trail through our block's wild interior practically a no-man's-land? Plus, I was sure that Pete, whose outdoor life seemed to consist mostly of sniffing the ground, would find this a wonderland of scents and tracks left by mice, raccoons, possum, cats, and other dogs. Surely, after a few visits, I thought, he'd be dragging me in there at every opportunity.

Once unclipped, Pete became a vague shadow, which freed me from any knowledge of what he was doing back there. We walked slowly past the old garages with their rickety carriage-house doors beneath tall fir trees that creaked in the wind. Sometimes the mud made sucking sounds as I lifted my feet. Honestly, the place was a little spooky. My son, Alex, who accompanied me once and gripped my hand for the entire trip, declined all further invitations.

Back out on the sidewalk, however, thinking Pete's business done, I'd be surprised to see him squatting in a curbside leaf pile or at the base of someone's hedges. What had he been doing there in the alley? Was it all so fascinating that he simply forgot to go? Didn't he understand that that was the point of going in there?

One night I brought a tiny pocket flashlight—a gift to Mr. Dog-walker from the kids. I wanted to see what Pete was doing in the dark. With its small light I could see him, off to my side. He didn't appear to be doing anything. He was simply walking, keeping pace with me. Toward the end of the lane, I watched him sniff at a wood-pile, at the massive base of a tree. His movements looked tentative. Something rattled in the woodpile. Pete headed for the exit and I was right behind him. Once out, he made a beeline for the pool of light beneath the street lamp. And there, in this heavily trafficked and visible area, he went into his squat. Cursing, I ransacked my pockets for a plastic bag.

That was how it went back there. Pete seemed as apprehensive as Alex with his vice-like grip on my hand. But at least Alex had an excuse: his imagination had been inflamed by horror movies and spooky stories. Sometimes, after a scary movie, I'd hear him running between the bathroom and his bedroom, as if something might catch him in the hall. But what could Pete be afraid of? He didn't read Stephen King or watch slasher movies. He saw better in the dark than I did. Wouldn't he see this place adjacent to our backyard in commonsense animal terms?

For a while, I persisted in taking him back there. I even tried singing songs to relax him. *Whistling past the graveyard!* But he kept an eye on me, and if I as much as leaned toward the entrance, he'd be out on the street and back to his favorite, well-lighted place.

I had to face it. My dog was afraid of the dark. Or at least afraid of pooping in the dark. I'd read somewhere that animals were instinctively uneasy at that moment lest something sneak up on them. Pete, in human terms, feared being caught with his pants down.

You have to love dog walking sometimes for the predicaments it puts you in. Of course, it was my own fault. As my wife said, "Wouldn't it be easier just to pick it up?"

Well, no.

Which is not to say that I don't admire those, like the young woman on 86th Street, who do this job with such grace and dignity. I don't think people get enough credit for doing something so contrary to human nature. We are always praising dogs' faithfulness and devotion, but what about human loyalty and devotion? Every day, dog walkers overcome deeply ingrained aversions and social embarrassment to perform this unpleasant job. After all, how many of us would put our spouses in a nursing home before we would do something like that for them?

In which case, I should be grateful for a wife who has such high ethics in these matters.

CHAPTER FIVE

Sniffing

In the hilly, irregular street pattern of my neighborhood, there is a place where two streets come together at a long, pointy angle. Because the houses that occupy this point face the street on the uphill side, there is a 150-foot sidewalk outside their supervisory range. This made it popular with dog walkers, some of whom were even less ethical than I was about picking up.

Pete sniffed and snorted the length of the grassy strip. From time to time, he would look up—like a scholar pulling his head out of a book. And then—not at all like a scholar—lift his leg and carefully urinate on the spot that he had just sniffed.

Like every dog owner, I knew that dogs had keen noses. I knew, too, that dogs, especially males, marked their territory and communicated with one another this way. I understood the interest in smelling. What came as a surprise was the *intensity* of that interest.

Pete's appraisal began with rapid-fire snuffling, progressed to excited scratching, and culminated with what looked like an attempt to dive headfirst into the scent. When he sniffed too long, I'd give a series of small, polite tugs on the leash. Finally, I'd attempt to pull him away only to discover that I couldn't budge him. *What the hell was so interesting down there?*

Once, Pete and I had a pulling contest because I tried to walk on the same side of the street we had just walked on. He kept yanking me toward the other side. I didn't get it at first. The view was the same. There were no dogs he wanted to meet over there. Finally it dawned on me: that was the unsniffed side.

It bothered me that Pete wasn't more interested in the obviously superior visual world that I enjoyed. We'd be walking along and I'd be admiring the wide and beautiful world—the clouds, the birds flitting between the trees, the squirrel twitching its tail on the tree trunk. From some vantage points, I could gaze for miles across the valley, past highways and towns—all the way out to the pale blue Watchung Mountains. A vista worthy of a Flemish landscape painter.

And where was Pete?

Walking with his nose stuck to the ground. If I tried to point things out to him, he would, like all dogs, stare at the end of my finger.

Yet I couldn't write off Pete's olfactory world so easily. He gave every sign of sorting through subtle and complex phenomena. He enjoyed smelling, I told myself, just as I enjoyed looking. Didn't I behave similarly in museums—pausing and studying various artworks, some with greater interest than others?

This was a time, I should mention, when the "dog culture" was still nascent. Average dog owners weren't as sophisticated about dog behavior as they are today. They hadn't heard yet about dogs' "hidden lives." They weren't conversant on subjects like "dominance hierarchies" and "canine scent-communication." Such information was still safely locked away in libraries. People had faith that their dogs were simple and straightforward animals.

I came home from the library with three or four books.

Is it just me, or does the thought of a big dog's nose—especially as a serious subject of study—make you slightly giddy? It's such an incredibly florid sense organ—so twitchy and curious and so prominent in the dog's physiognomy—as if to proclaim: "Sniffing is all!"

The first author began with a tour of the nose. I followed him through the dark portal and allowed myself to be whisked into the depths like the miniature submarine in *Fantastic Voyage*. I gazed on the mountainous landscape of the dog's convoluted nasal membrane. My notes from the time capture my wonderment: "If flattened out, the dog's nasal membrane would cover an area the size of a queen-size bed!" And, "220 million waving cilia compared to a mere 5 million for humans!" And, "Nasal mucous must be replenished at a rate of 1¾ gallons a day!"

All this equipment translates into a very sensitive nose. Estimates varied from a nose 1,000 times more sensitive than a human's to, in the case of the bloodhound, an astonishing "100 million times" more sensitive.

Some of the experiments carried out to test the acuity of the dog's nose sound like the result of barroom bets. My favorite, conducted by the United States Army, tested a group of beagles' ability to track a man across a grassy field. In the first test, the man crossed the field with bare feet. The next was a little harder: following the trail of a man who had worn rubber boots. Next was the trail of a man who rode a bicycle across the field. In the grand finale, the field was plowed, doused with gasoline, and set on fire. After it was put out, the dogs still picked up the scent.

None of this prepared me for the next revelation: Dogs have a second olfactory system within the first. This other nose, the vomeronasal organ, is believed to respond exclusively to the airborne hormones called pheromones.

Using these two noses, a dog can put together quite a dossier on another. From scent alone comes information as to a dog's sex, age, state of health, consanguity, and—if female—readiness for sex.

Scientists cheerfully discuss this behavior in such terms as "airborne aphrodisiacs," "canine calling cards," and "scent-telephones," which ignores how fundamentally strange and beyond our understanding all this is. The bottom line is that you're completely out of the loop. You're up on your hind legs, away from the ground, with your pathetically atrophied olfactory system, lamely admiring the scenery while your dog is answering a personal ad for "a hot stud who's looking for a good time."

When I shared such information with friends, I invariably got the same reaction. All were impressed with the dog's olfactory powers, but none envied it. No one seemed interested in exchanging their nose for one a hundred-million times more sensitive. This would seem to stem from a human conviction that there are too many bad smells out there and not enough good ones.

People also have a hard time imagining the dog's olfactory heaven—enjoying a scent so much that they'd fight to keep their noses in it. We're not even capable of such sustained smelling. All humans have a built-in short-circuiting mechanism called habitu-ation that cuts off the response after a few sniffs. Good or bad, the smell starts to fade.

Not dogs. They can —and do—sniff and sniff and sniff without any diminished sensation.

Still, you might expect them to get bored after a while. Why do they continue to enjoy this endless sniffing? What do they get out of it? Years ago, Pete had a strange reaction to a scent he picked up near a fire hydrant. He recoiled in a slow-motion, spooky way, as if in deference to a powerful, malignant force. For weeks, he gave this place a wide berth. I found this fascinating. How could a smell—or just the memory of one—be so disturbing? I've encountered smells I'd prefer to avoid, but none that scared me.

Scientists say some scents—those carrying pheromones—can stimulate a dog's emotions directly. "Odors play tunes in the dog's brain," writes the British veterinarian Bruce Fogle. He proceeds to describe scents that act as "hidden persuaders," that cause "mood shifts," or even "physiological changes to the central nervous system . . ."

I began to understand why Pete would linger over a smell so long—or be so frightened by one. While I was innocently watching the clouds or enjoying the sight of a squirrel shaking its tail, he was having something akin to a drug experience.

Who knew?

CHAPTER SIX

Groundhog Day

Dog walking has a dark side. Every dog walker knows this. For all its potential to take you beyond ordinary concerns, to restore your simpler self and put you in harmony with the natural world, it can occasionally lead to boredom, déjà vu, ennui, anomie, alienation, depression, and, in extreme cases, outright despair.

I was a few years into my dog-walking career when I fell into my funk. At the time, some people (namely my wife) thought I was having a midlife crisis. Perhaps I was. I was forty-five, ripe for that sort of thing.

> *Nel mezzo del cammin di nostra vita*
> *Mi ritrovai per una selva oscura*
>
> *(In the middle of our life's journey*
> *I found myself lost in a dark wood.)*
>
> —Dante Alighieri, Canto One of *The Inferno*

Looking back, I can see the confluence of life issues that led to this. Strangely enough, they all involved the problem of repetitiveness, by which I mean that uncomfortable and sometimes hellish experience when the same stupid things seem to be happening over and over again. And these problems flowed into dog-walking's empty vessel at a time when it had taken on an extremely repetitive character.

Let's start with the dog-walking part. To be at all satisfying, dog walking requires an engagement with the world. If you fail to put that energy and imagination into it, routine gets the upper hand. Gradually, you cede control of the walk to your more purposeful partner. This tree or that, it's all the same to you. Does the tail wag the dog?

People tend to blame the resulting tedium on the dog. The dog, they like to say, is a creature of habit. But as we have seen, the dog's "habits" have a secret content, an olfactory world of evocative scents and intoxicating pheromones. Subjectively, my dog's perusals of the grassy strip were filled with spice and variety. He checked his social calendar, noted the arrival of newcomers to the area, engaged in flirtations, boasted of his virility and readiness to mate, obliterated similar claims by rival males, and carried on extended arguments with such rivals as to who was "top dog" and who was "a quivering puppy about to urinate on himself."

I, on the other hand, had nothing in the way of messages on the grassy strip except for the recyclables and household goods my neighbors brought out to the curb. Dog walking affords extended opportunities to study this stuff, and it has its small rewards. You can learn that your neighbor has given up on his exercise bike or tossed out his golf clubs, that someone finally got

tired of saving all those *National Geographics*, that this one sub-
scribes to the left-leaning *Nation* or that one to the right-leaning
National Review, that the neighbor's twins have graduated from
their bunk beds, that so-and-so just got a 60-inch television, and
finally, most revealingly, how much and what kind of liquor your
neighbors drink. Nevertheless, this is all thin gruel compared to
what a dog is picking up.

Around the time this all started, the theme of tedious repetition
had seeped into my job, as well. I was getting head-numbing jolts
of déjà vu from contemporary art. These frustrations came to rest
on Andy Warhol, who, though already dead by this time, continued
to grow in reputation. Warhol was probably the first artist in history to produce art that was *intentionally* dull and repetitious. Years
before, there had issued forth from his studio—his "factory"—repli-
cas of Brillo boxes and Campbell Soup cans, stamp-sheet images of
Mao and Marilyn and other duplications. *You want repetitiveness?* he
seemed to ask. *I'll give you repetitiveness. How about an eight-hour film
of a man sleeping? Or an all-night view of the Empire State building?* Art
critics turned themselves inside out trying to explain the profound
philosophical questions that Warhol was raising.

Reading an article about Warhol in *Newsweek* you might shake
your head and chuckle. *Oh, what a devilish character, that Warhol! Always turning everything on its head!* But going to exhibit after
exhibit—both of his work and those just like him—the irony of his
tediousness wore off and became just . . . tedious.

In life, Warhol had looked like an apparition—that expres-
sionless face, the bloodless pallor, the blank eyes, the mouth that

rarely moved. In death, he *was* an apparition. And the apparition demanded publicity. Posthumous stories had to be written about his will, his diary, the auction, the Andy Warhol Foundation, the Andy Warhol retrospectives. This went on for years.

"I like boring things," Warhol had said. "I like things to be the same over and over."

My dog couldn't have said it better. Pete and I were marching around the block like two pieces on a giant Monopoly board. Twice a day, we'd come out the front door, advance to the sidewalk's first square, and go *Bink! Bink! Bink!* around the board. Roll the dice! *Bink! Bink! Bink! Bink!* The dog pees on the tree, the same tree as this morning, as last night, as last week, as the week before.

I tried taking up a pipe, thinking it might bestow some reflective dignity on these duties. I found a corncob one at the drugstore. It worked for a while. It melded with the stop-and-start rhythms of the dog walk, since it was always going out and I was always having to re-light and get it stoking again, but it was a mere Band-Aid for my troubled soul.

Sometimes I felt like I'd been assigned a Zen problem by a sadistic master.

Look again at this well-trodden sidewalk, this familiar tree, this same sequence of houses, this empty lot. . . . Now do you understand?

Uh, no.

Return tomorrow!

Naturally, I reflected on the repetitive hells of mythology. Good old Sisyphus, rolling his rock up the hill over and over again, seemed like a kindred spirit. And poor Prometheus, the tragic Titan who was condemned by Zeus to have his ever-regenerating liver plucked out by an eagle every day for all of eternity. Why is never-ending repetition such a popular feature of so many imagined hells? Is repetition of the same torment worse than a sequence of different torments? Or is it just too taxing on the human imagination to conceive of an eternity of different punishments? Or an eternity of anything?

Around that time, I saw the movie *Groundhog Day*. In this strangely serious comedy, a bored and cynical weatherman named Phil Collins (played by Bill Murray) is sent on assignment to Punxsutawney, Pennsylvania, for an annual Groundhog Day ceremony. There, by some mysterious act of Providence, he is compelled to repeat this same day (with minor variations) over and over and over again. I watched, transfixed, as this seemingly kindred spirit writhed on the hook of his own bland Hell.

Was I so very different? Phil the weatherman had his groundhog, and I had . . . Pete.

With the endless vacuity of dog walking stretching ahead of me like a bleak surrealist landscape, I did what any man would do in this situation. I complained to my wife.

"I think I need some time out," I said after dinner one night. "A respite."

"From what?" Janet asked.

"You know . . ." I nodded at Pete, who was lying on the kitchen floor, dark eyes fixed on me, waiting to leap to his feet the moment I uttered one of the magic words: "dog," "walk," or "out."

"Really?" said Janet. "I thought you liked . . . *that*."

I shrugged. There has always been an unacknowledged element of theater in these conversations with my wife, both of us playing our parts, neither quite sure how serious the other one is.

"Is this some sort of midlife crisis?"

"No," I said. "It's more like . . . *Groundhog Day*."

There followed a familiar discussion about who had to do what in the evenings and in the mornings—meals, dishes, bedtime preparation—and what time *some* people had to get to work compared to other people.

Even the discussion gave me a déjà vu.

In no time at all I was bested.

I fell into a long silence.

"Claire can take Peter after school," said Janet, throwing me a bone. "She does sometimes."

"I know, I know," I said. My daughter, like most modern children, had a busy schedule: Brownie meetings, piano lessons, sports, play rehearsals. More to the point, however, was that the afternoon dog walk was purely recreational and therefore irrelevant to the problem. It provided no respite from the hygienically essential morning and evening walks.

Janet took a sip of tea and looked at the clock. I tried a different tack.

"How much time do you think I spend at this W-A-L-K-I-N-G thing?"

Pete's tail began tapping an insistent rhythm on the floor. Somehow, even without the code words, he was getting the drift. Dogs sense these things.

I refilled my wineglass and looked at him defiantly.

"Let's figure it out," I said, suddenly curious to know the real answer. I dug a calculator out of the kitchen junk drawer. "Let's say that I put in a half hour in the morning and a half hour in the evening." I was aware that I was talking a bit too excitedly. "That's the bare minimum. There are no days off, so that comes to seven hours a week, or 365 hours annually, right?"

Janet got up to load the dishwasher.

"How long do these . . . *canine companions* live?" I asked.

She shrugged. "Maybe fifteen years."

"Let's say twelve years, to be conservative," I said, punching the numbers into the calculator. "That's a total of . . . 4,380 hours."

"Uh-huh," said my wife.

"Doesn't that sound like a lot?" I asked.

"I don't know. I'd have to know how much of my life I spend loading and unloading the dishwasher."

"We sleep a third of our lives," I said. "My job takes up another third. What else is left?"

"A third?"

"No," I said. "I have to deduct for . . . you know . . ."

I was punching more numbers into the calculator. I divided 4,380 hours by an average 37½-hour workweek to get a sense of how many "work hours" this "job" involved.

"Two years!" I said. "A two-year career of you-know-what."

"I really think you're having a midlife crisis," said Janet.

"I'm not having a midlife crisis," I said.

"So what *are* you having?"

"I'm having a *dog-walking* crisis."

Pete jumped to his feet.

"Uh-oh," said Janet, as Pete began his mad celebratory dance. "You said the secret word."

CHAPTER SEVEN

The Fringe

In time, Pete and I broke out of our rut. Everyone does, sooner or later, even the main character in *Groundhog Day*. In fact, that was one of the things—on a serious level—that I liked about the movie: the character doesn't achieve wisdom as a result of sudden insight, deep meditation, or religious conversion. His conceits and self-centered desires are simply ground away by near-ceaseless repetition (according to an interview with the screenwriter, Danny Rubin, Phil the weatherman endured 10,000 Groundhog Days—or about twenty-eight years' worth).

Like him, I think I simply exhausted my self-preoccupation, one layer at a time. Dog walking is good for that. You don't become enlightened or discover any state of grace. But it opens up two slots in your life in which you confront the same basic reality over and over again.

I stopped fretting over the Culture Wars, about Andy Warhol, about midlife crises, and about how many hours I spent walking the dog.

The dog-walking part of the problem was solved, rather simply, by finding a new, more interesting place to walk. It was one of those little "preserves" that suburban towns sometimes have.

There wasn't much to this place, really—just a dozen acres or so of third- or fourth-growth forest. Coming in, you could see clear through to the other side, to another suburban neighborhood in the adjacent town. It seemed not so much a forest as an interruption, as if the development machine had hit a bump and left this patch raw.

That's pretty much what had happened. The land had been slated for development, but a citizens group—alarmed that the town was about to lose its last piece of woodland—organized, lobbied, wrote letters, went to town council meetings, and eventually got a "Green Acres" grant. The land was saved.

A newly formed environmental commission took charge and installed wood-chip trails, railroad-tie steps, footbridges, botanical labels, and, the crowning touch—an elegant timber-and-laminate sign worthy of a national park.

Thinking about it now, I'm reminded again of those walled-in sanctuaries in the medieval illuminations I liked, but in a different way. They told a story of wilderness menacing civilization. Now the situation was reversed: It was civilization menacing forest.

Having created this sanctuary for the natural world, the community seemed to forget exactly what they had in mind to do with it. It was like an heirloom—valuable, but of no real use. Earlier generations had a relationship with the forest, even if it was an antagonistic one. But contemporary suburbanites had no such relationship. To have one, they had to believe in something, such as the spiritual benefits of communing with nature. In other words, they needed a philosophy. Or a dog.

In those days, there didn't even seem to be that many dog walkers around. Pete and I pretty much had the place to ourselves.

As small as these woods were, the network of trails created an illusion of space, and along a few stretches, civilization dropped entirely from view. A couple of streams trickled lethargically down the hill. Shrubby dogwoods clung to the steepest places. Vines snaked up tree trunks and dangled down over the trails. Slender oaks and sweet gums shot up sixty feet before sending out a horizontal branch.

At the top of the hill, the trees stopped abruptly at a retaining wall, beyond which was a shopping center. Debris and litter came over this fence. Feral cats straddled the two worlds, making nighttime forays over the fence to hunt or scavenge in dumpsters. At night, the mercury-vapor security lamps shone an eerie, orange light through the trees.

The place had a mood. My kids nicknamed it the "Mystery Trails," a joke, really, because the overeager environmentalists had created so many trail choices that, upon entering, you felt like a character on a Tarot card. But it did have its share of mystery. All woods do, I think, because they are naturally concealing, and sometimes disorienting, places. You're never sure what's around you in the woods, and you're never sure exactly where you are. Even in the modern world, forests swallow people up.

Of course, this wasn't really a forest, nor would I call it a "nature preserve." It had trees, but it was more like something I remembered from childhood: a fringe place.

To understand the origins of the fringe, you have to go all the way back to that day in the middle of the nineteenth century, July 4, 1845, when Thoreau moved into his cabin on the shores of Walden Pond in Concord. He lived there simply, and in relative solitude, for two years and two months. He read, worked on books, wrote in his journal, chopped wood, tended a garden, fished, and took lots and lots of walks. He tried to open himself up to everything around him—the pond, the woods, the animals, and the passage of the seasons.

On his third day at Walden, he wrote in his journal, "I wish to meet the facts of life—the vital facts, which were the phenomena or actuality the Gods meant to show us—face to face. And so I came down here. Life! Who knows what it is—what it does?"

At the time, it wasn't unusual for artists and intellectuals like Thoreau to immerse themselves in nature. Herman Melville spent four years at sea. Thomas Cole and his Hudson River School followers traipsed all over the continent in search of breathtakingly wild and primitive scenery. As it happened, my walks around these tiny woods corresponded with a revival of interest in these pictures. Forgotten during a half-century of modernist revolutions, the Hudson River School was enjoying a second life in the New York museums. These artists had looked longer and harder at the natural world in its wilder aspects than any group before or since. Their aesthetic grew out of an American pantheism, a belief that powerful, primeval forces could bring you closer to God. Like an aesthetic thrill ride, their paintings tried to get you to that tricky place where grandeur met fear and trembling, an aesthetic response they called the *sublime*.

Thoreau believed no less that the divine could be experienced through the medium of nature, but he had a different take. He wasn't looking for the spectacular or the scary. Nor did he go to Walden in search of *adventure*. Nor was he a hermit in the wilderness. His cabin was only about 500 yards from the embankment of the Fitchburg Railroad. Walking on its tracks, he could get to town in about twenty minutes. He wanted to demonstrate that this way of life—this experiment in living that he was carrying out—could be done anywhere, by anyone. A person had only to step a bit off center, had only to find a rough spot *on the fringe*.

When I think of Walden Woods I don't think of it as the shrine for nature worshippers that it's become. I think of it as America's first fringe place. And the spirit that impelled Thoreau there was not so far from that of the boy who sneaks away to build a tree house in the woods near his house.

One reason I like the fringe is that unusual things happen there. Years later, walking in another place, more wild and neglected than the woods, I spotted a white vial at the side of the path. It was plastic, the kind of small bottle that Tylenol or aspirin comes in. I picked it up. It had no labels and no top, but someone had written with a black marker: "Don't Throw Out." When I turned it over, the other side said "Diamonds."

Hah! What was this? A joke?

I lingered, musing and turning the thing over in my hand. Pete came over to see what was what. I let him sniff the vial. *Lead me to the diamonds, Lassie!*

I confess that I put one eye to the vial and looked in. And, yes, I looked down at my feet to the place where I had picked up the bottle, perchance to see some telltale sparkle in the grass. And, yes, I even bent over for a second to peer more closely among the blades. *They could have been diamond chips.* . . . Pete, of course, gave it the once-over, sniffing so vigorously that anything less than a quarter carat would have disappeared into his capacious nose.

In the end I brought the bottle home and put it on the bookshelf above my computer as a reminder. Of what, exactly? Of the wonderful randomness and illogic of events on the fringe.

At the time of Thoreau's experiment the fringe was generous and close at hand—a ring around every city and town. A little more than a century later, when I was growing up in the suburbs, it had been reduced to a patchwork of woods, meadows, unbuildable swamps, empty lots, old quarries, abandoned coal yards, and former railroad stops. And now the pieces were even smaller. Suburbs blended into other suburbs without any buffer between. Pete and I were lucky to find this sliver. What we found looked very much like the kinds of woods I had played in as a child.

The only difference was that this one had a sign and a license to exist. It was something new: a sanctioned fringe place.

Soon, bored by our repetitive circuits and made somewhat dreamy by the woods' flickering light, I slipped into fantasies of the frontier. These drew on information gleaned from a variety of random sources: museum dioramas, the novels of James Fenimore Cooper, the paintings of Thomas Cole, and history talks at the local library. I pictured the indigenous Leni Lenape longhouses, Magua, Hawkeye, French soldiers, and the Kaaterskill Falls. I became wary, alert to the slightest stirring in the brush; I listened suspiciously to the calls of birds. I stepped over dry leaves, never snapped a stick. I studied the trail for tracks, and conferred with my wolf-dog, Lupo.

I'd study a broken branch and imagine myself saying: "This looks fresh, Lupo. No more than four or five hours ago."

I'd spot a tiny scrap of fabric caught on a thorn bush. *It's calico! They must have taken the women!"*

Pete could be induced to cooperate in this game as long as he didn't know it was a game. He'd quicken his pace if I quickened mine, and he'd put his nose to the ground if I pointed there and acted interested.

But if I spoke out loud, if I said, in my Hawkeye voice, *"Which way, Lupo?"* he'd woof in annoyance, the way he did when the kids put on their Halloween costumes. His sense of humor didn't extend to costumes, wigs, funny voices, impersonations, or any other identity-altering behaviors. He expected his human companions to always be themselves—just as he was.

As it turned out, the "Mystery Trails" had actual mysteries, after all.

I was awakened from my games of pretend one early spring morning by a pair of black lace panties. They dangled from the lower branch of a sweet gum tree. I stopped and stared. The panties fluttered a little in the breeze. They had not been there yesterday. Someone had come to the woods in the night and left without her underwear.

I tried to imagine the circumstances behind such a lapse. I was forced to conclude that these familiar woods of mine, through which I tramped every morning and which I tried to enliven with my *Last of the Mohicans* fantasies, had revealed its true character. It was a dark wood, filled with feverish desires and hoarse whispers.

The panties remained there for several days, then disappeared. I took them as a harbinger of spring. I had discovered these woods in winter and had traipsed about them during the "off season," so to speak. Now, it was as if the sprites and wood nymphs were coming out of a long winter's sleep, except these ephemeral presences didn't use dandelion parasols and drink from buttercups. They left empty six-packs, 40-ounce Colt 45 bottles, Marlboro cigarette boxes, and plastic spheres called "beer bubbles."

I began to realize that the same lack of authority that attracted me to this place attracted others with less innocent motives. One day I arrived to find a bunch of stumps where trees had been. Following the happy hour, perhaps, some juvenile delinquents had gotten busy with an ax and felled about a dozen sweet gum trees. The ax lay discarded on the ground amidst the chips and fallen trunks.

I was furious at first. What right had they? And yet, on reflection, I could understand. It was a ritual, a right of passage. You spit on both palms. You swing the ax. Chips fly. *Tim-ber!* What did I expect from the fringe?

But the scar looked ugly, and when I came back, it looked the same. Even those unimpressive trees, I realized, were probably thirty or forty years old. I'd be tree fertilizer myself before this piece of forest was returned to the state it had been in the day before.

The funny thing was that I never actually saw any of these activities firsthand. It was like an unofficial timeshare arrangement. They were the shadow people.

I began to approach my dog walks with a certain anthropological curiosity. Up on the high ground was a race of fort builders who made primitive enclosures by lashing together stockade-size logs. Watching their improvements was like seeing the progress of civilization. One week they were squatting on the ground, the next week they were sitting on a discarded Barcalounger.

My favorites were the dam builders. They had to make do with a barely trickling stream, but working diligently, using big rocks, and packing the gaps with sticks and mud, they caused a small, muddy pond to appear. When Pete took to wallowing in it, I was forced to become a saboteur. I tried to be principled, removing only a key rock or two to restore the flow. This, I remembered from my own childhood, came with the territory. We were forever building things and threatening, "Nobody better wreck this," knowing of course, that somebody would. And if they didn't, *we* would, just so we could rebuild it.

A day or two later, the dam was whole again. I gazed down at the repair work and smiled. I pictured them rushing here after school to see what Mr. Dam-wrecker had done.

Then I realized. I was one of them now. I was somebody else's other. One of the shadow people.

Chapter Eight

Tethered

The woods changed everything. Pete no longer dawdled over scents on the grassy strip, no longer malingered at the bases of trees while I stood around wondering what to do with myself. He was too busy yanking me down the street.

He loved those woods. Whether this was because he could run free off the leash, or because the pheromones were more intoxicating there, or because of an instinctive response to a place that resembled the primeval forest of his wolfish ancestors, I can't say. All I knew was that he wanted to get there and viewed me as an inconvenient anchor.

I can still hear him ventilating and panting, like a whole team of sled dogs. He was surprisingly strong for a poodle. It was hard to believe that he could tug me so easily. I felt like a subject in a jujitsu demonstration. Pete, only sixty-five pounds but equipped with four legs to my two and a much lower center of gravity, could pull me in whatever direction he chose.

Dogs, I've since learned, love to pull. In fact, they excel at it as a sport. People take their dogs to meets, where the dogs—big ones like Saint Bernards and Newfoundlands—are harnessed to oversize pickup trucks, which they must pull from a dead stop. The world record in this competition is close to 6,000 pounds. I don't think Pete could have competed in that league, but he didn't have to. He didn't have to pull a three-ton pickup truck. All he had to pull was a 175-pound art critic.

Every time he surged, I'd be forced to make a series of small rapid steps to keep from falling on my face. I tried various countermeasures. I tried walking in a leaned-back position in order to increase drag, but it was uncomfortable and ineffective.

I tried stern words. I tried slaps on the rear end. But again and again I was reduced to the comical figure of a man tripping and stumbling behind his dog. I would have been firmer had the whole thing not seemed so funny and had I not, on some level, identified with his willful eagerness to get to the woods.

As any dog trainer will tell you, the solution to the problem of a dog pulling on the leash is to teach the dog to heel. I know all about this.

My mother, a clinical psychologist, got a dog just before I went away to college. I was an only child, my mother was a single parent, and as is often the case with parents facing an empty nest, she was looking for something to fill the gap. After a great deal of research, she settled on a female Welsh terrier puppy that she named Megan. Megan was brown and black with those bushy terrier whiskers and eyebrows.

As a puppy, Megan was cute and playful. But people often don't understand what they are getting with a pedigree dog. Welsh terriers, for example, were bred to go into burrows after badgers. It's a nasty business. Badgers are tough. They have broad backs, thick, short legs, and long digging claws on their front feet. They can be fierce when harassed or cornered. The men who bred these terriers—called "terrier men"—would probably be arrested for animal cruelty today. They would send the terrier down into the badger's den to flush it out. The dog had to be small enough to get into the burrow, which meant that it had no size advantage over its adversary, and the fights were ferocious. The terrier would either kill the badger, be killed itself, or fight the badger to some sort of stand-off—meaning both animals would be exhausted and wounded, in which case the terrier man would dig down with a shovel and shoot the badger.

The dog bred for this kind of work had to make up for its small size with raw courage, aggressiveness, and stubbornness. It was no lap dog.

My mother knew all this. She had, as I said, researched everything. But, like many people, her choice of a dog wasn't really a rational one. I believe she was taken with the idea of a dog that was small and pixyish, but also feisty—like her.

When I came home from college for the first time during Thanksgiving holiday, my mother and Megan had finished obedience school training. My mother had taken the classes very seriously. Megan had been the class valedictorian. The graduation pictures, along with the diploma and small mortarboard cap the dog had been given, were professionally framed and displayed on the wall of the living room. Already Megan had surpassed my accomplishments.

Later, we went out to walk the dog. Megan, on a taut, short lead, inscribed an arc in front of us, her feet scrambling on the concrete pavement.

I started talking about college, but before I finished my first sentence I was interrupted by a cry of "Heel!"

I waited until my mother brought the dog back to the proper position before I tried resuming the conversation.

I got out another sentence or two before it happened again.

The pattern continued. The dog would comply for maybe thirty seconds. Then her enthusiasm would get the better of her, and she'd drift ahead a bit. Then my mother would bark like a drill instructor and yank her back in line, and so on.

I asked her if all this was really necessary.

"There's nothing cruel about this," she said, ready to head off any sentimental pleas on behalf of the dog. She went on to explain the mechanism of a choke collar. "It doesn't really choke her," she said. "It just gives her a good, hard pinch. A negative reinforcement."

A succession of good hard pinches didn't sound like such a picnic to me. More to the point, I thought my mother was destroying the spirit of their outing, turning it into something repressive instead of fun.

"She's like a kid," I said. "She likes to run ahead. What's the harm?"

"This is what they teach them in obedience school," my mother said. "The dog is supposed to walk next to the owner, without tugging on the leash."

My mother launched into the classic explanation of dog pack behavior and hierarchies.

"A dog that insists on walking in front is asserting its dominance," she said. "That's the position of the alpha dog, the leader of the pack. When it runs ahead like that, it's saying, 'I'm the alpha dog!' You see? It's an attempt at dominance."

Perhaps I was only annoyed that her overzealous discipline was making it impossible for us to have a conversation, but I told her that it seemed ridiculous to imagine that this dog, which weighed about fifteen pounds, stood less than a foot high, and was roped around its neck, could have any illusions of dominance.

"Anyway, what does it matter what the dog thinks?" I asked.

"Oh," said my mother, playing the psychologist card, "you have an identification issue with this dog." Then she yelled "Heel!" once more, and yanked so hard on the lead that Megan's front feet came off the ground.

Megan learned to heel, I guess, but the relationship didn't go well. Perhaps it was Megan's terrier genes. Her type wasn't bred to give in, and my mother was equally determined to be the alpha dog. All the conflict and frustration seemed to make Megan neurotic. She started growling and snapping at people's feet. On top of all this, my mother expected Megan to be a lap dog. She'd hoist this fierce little terrier up onto her lap and begin to stroke her head. Megan's body would tense up and gradually you'd hear her growling.

"She's purring," my mother would say, still stroking Megan's head. With each stroke, the dog would show her teeth a little more and growl a little louder. When the tension became unbearable, Megan would explode with a loud bark, jump down off my mother's lap, and run to the corner. There she would sit, head down and growling, miserable with guilt.

A few years later, my mother took Megan to see a dog psychologist, but by then it was apparently too late. Whatever therapy they tried didn't work. Megan was set in her ways. My mother accepted it. And they grew old together.

So it was that example—admittedly an extreme case—turned me off to the whole practice of heeling dogs. I still wince a little whenever I see someone jerking his dog's collar and shouting "Heel! Heel!"

I've seen dogs that heel gracefully. They walk next to the owner, the leash hanging without any tension, a symbol of the harmony that exists between them. But I still don't like it. The dog always looks like it's walking on tiptoes.

Dog books do a lot of mischief, I think, with all this "dominance" and alpha-dog talk. It's one thing to say that a dog that growls and snaps at a woman's boyfriend is trying to be dominant. It's another to say, as one book of mine does, that a dog that stares at you because he wants to go out is trying to be dominant.

I never bothered over the "alpha-dog" theory. I didn't think Pete saw me as a dog, much less a subordinate one, or that we were in any kind of power struggle for hierarchy points. Pete could be pretty stubborn, and there were times, I knew, where he questioned my judgment. But so what? There were times when he was right. Just as there were times when I was right. We disagreed on the speed with which we should proceed to the woods, and here he clearly got a bit carried away.

He could have been more mindful of me, I suppose, but then again, it was never Pete's idea—or any dog's—that he be tethered to a human and forced to coordinate movements, like a partner in a silly three-legged race.

And, truth be told, I wasn't any more comfortable with it than he was. Not enough has been written in those training books on humans who don't take to the leash. I didn't want to be tied to him, either, and I certainly wouldn't want to be forced to mince along while he barked at me to heel.

CHAPTER NINE

Found Object

Dogs have a habit of picking up disgusting things. Their noses guide them to odiferous dead fish, chicken carcasses, pork ribs, lumps of horse manure, dirty underwear, soggy socks. Worse, once they've got something like that, you often have to get it out of their mouths.

One day, walking in the woods, I noticed that Pete had in his mouth what looked suspiciously like a type of sex toy. It was phallic and made of a black rubbery plastic.

"Pete," I said, "Come here, boy."

He trotted over to me, his head bobbing. He knew that he had something unusual and interesting. He came just close enough for me to confirm what it was.

"Oh, Jesus," I said. "Where did you get that?"

He wagged his tail, then veered away.

"Come here, Pete," I said, trying to sound as if the matter I wished to see him about had nothing to do with that thing in his mouth. "Come on, boy."

He wasn't fooled. He went into his play-bow, tail wagging, chin on his paws.

"Pete," I said. "I'm not going to chase you."

Just chase me a little, his response said. He dropped the toy on the ground in front of him. When I didn't take the bait, he tried to make it more enticing by nudging it a little with his nose. He was like some cardsharp luring in a sucker—because, of course, I had absolutely no chance of snatching that thing away from him. I had learned a few things about this game since Pete first introduced me to it.

In the beginning, like all dog owners, I played fetch with my dog. I would toss the stick as far as I could, and he would run after it, pick it up, and bring it back to me. But after a while, his interest waned.

Soon he taught me a variation: tug-of-war.

Then he taught me another: keep-away.

I know there are dog disciplinarians out there who are tsking at my failure to enforce the rules of fetch as befitting the alpha-master, but fair is fair and Pete had a point. Fetch was less a game than a cooperative recreation. Tug-of-war, in comparison, was a contest requiring strength, grit, and determination. It had a winner and a loser. There were lots of groans and growls and digging in of heels and paws. To even have a chance of prevailing, I had to get two hands on the object and use all the torque I could muster to wrest it out of his jaws.

Keep-away required agility and lightning-fast reflexes. In this game, I was the clumsy bull and Pete was the matador. He never moved more than was precisely necessary to evade my grasp.

That was the position I was in now, as Pete danced around in front of me with this absurd thing, this—no point in being delicate—*dildo* in his jaws. He was ready for sport.

"Pete," I said sternly. "This is not a game. Bring that thing over here."

He leaned forward in his play-bow position, then leapt gaily away into another play-bow. For him, this was what really made the game: when I actually wanted the thing he possessed.

It was an absurd predicament, hilarious really, and yet, beneath it all, I was shocked. What was this community of mine coming to when a dog could pick up a dildo in the woods? The offbeat charms of the fringe notwithstanding, you worry about such things when you're raising kids in a community.

Pete's bark brought me back to my immediate problem. Impatient for me to chase him, he was tapping the phallic toy around with one paw, as if to trick me into thinking it was alive.

I couldn't let him run around with this thing. After all, what if someone else walked into the woods and saw us? What if it was a mother and a young child? What exactly would I say? I sized up my opponent. Pete was getting more extravagant in his efforts to animate his prize. Now he was tossing it up in the air. Even through that furry face I could see the mischievous glint in his eyes.

I saw a chance to get it if I could startle him. To throw him off guard, I pretended to be studying something up in the trees. Then, I turned and charged him, bellowing like a bull.

His eyes showed their whites all the way around and his legs seemed to bend like rubber. But he twisted away from me and when the dust cleared he still had his prize.

I had only one more ruse. I put my hands in my jacket pockets and went off down the path. By and by, his feet came padding behind me. I silently counted to three, then whirled around and grabbed him by the collar. I scissored him between my legs and wrenched open his jaws. The contested object rolled out of his mouth onto the ground.

I held Pete by the collar to keep him from seizing it again. Now, in addition to all the other disincentives for handling this thing, it was covered with dog saliva. I forced myself to fetch it. As I quickly thrust it above my head, out of Pete's reach, I must have hit a switch, because the thing went on.

There I was, in my moment of triumph: a man standing in the woods, in a pose reminiscent of the Statue of Liberty, holding a vibrating dildo above his head.

CHAPTER TEN

Call of the Wild

One day Pete took off after a plastic shopping bag. We were on the broad central trail of the woods and a gust sent it skidding along the ground. It darted around until Pete pounced on it. Then he ran with it in his jaws, shaking the life out of it. He looked less like a predator than a caricature of one.

Another time, the bag chased him. We were approaching the woods at night and a thirty-three-gallon trash bag that someone had left on their lawn inflated in the wind and sent Pete scurrying into the street.

What would happen to him, I wondered, if he was turned loose in the wild and had to catch and eat his own food? Would he survive?

In Jack London's *The Call of the Wild*, the dog-hero, Buck, is living a lazy life on a California ranch when he is stolen and sold to gold traders in the Far North. He is turned into a sled dog and a fighting dog. He learns to use his instincts and cunning to survive. After a series of masters, some bad, some good, he finds himself free in the wild north. He meets a she-wolf and runs off to live the life of a wild animal with her.

White Fang is the opposite story. Here, the "dog" is a mostly wolf hybrid, born into a wolf pack. He is living wild in the same Far North where Buck ended up. He is caught and lives with Indians at first. Then he is sold to a white man, and, like Buck, becomes a fighting dog. Ultimately he is rescued by a kind master and brought to live on a ranch in California. There he proves his value to society by saving the family from an escaped convict.

In one story, a dog ends up living like a wolf, and in the other, a wolf ends up living like a dog. Both are happy endings. In London's world, animals—and humans—hear two siren calls: the call of the wild and the call of the mild.

For a long time, scientists were unsure which members of the canine family dogs had evolved from. The incredible range in size and appearance led some to speculate that dogs must have descended from more than one species. Konrad Lorenz thought they were part wolf, part jackal. Jackals are subservient animals compared to wolves, and this, he thought, would account for why some dogs—like my poodle—were so gentle. After all, how could a poodle be a near-wolf?

And yet, it practically is. Eventually DNA analysis proved that dogs have only one ancestor—the wolf—and that the two species have 99 percent of their genes in common. Dogs and wolves can still mate. Jack London's stories about the two species "crossing over" weren't so far off the mark.

Wolves have a better public image than they once did. We fret over dwindling wolf populations. Teachers describe wolves and coyotes as "wild dogs" so children will feel more positively about them. We watch nature films in which they are depicted as noble and beautiful animals. It's easy to forget that for thousands and thousands of years, people hated and despised wolves. They hunted them, shot them, trapped them, and poisoned them. They hung their skins up as trophies. The only reason there are any wolves left in the world is that the wolves retreated to mostly uninhabited areas and people decided not to pursue the war to its bitter conclusion.

So it's rather startling that such an animal—the so-called man-eating wolf of folklore and legend—could be rehabilitated, as it were, and celebrated with equal enthusiasm as "man's best friend." What creature has ever done such an about-face?

Once, on a family visit to the Museum of Natural History, we stopped in front of the wolf diorama in the Hall of North American Mammals. The scene is a snowy landscape at night. In the bluish moonlight, two timber wolves are running. Their pale eyes glow yellow. Their powerful bodies are frozen in mid-stride. They are on the hunt.

Here, I thought to myself, was the life that 99 percent of Pete's genes were designed for. It was a little hard to believe. After all, this was our person in a dog suit. He climbed up on our beds and, when he thought we weren't looking, put his head on the pillow. Meanwhile, buried somewhere in his brain were the circuits for killing and devouring the likes of us.

Although Pete had all the basic equipment of a wolf—teeth, claws, speed, intelligence—he didn't have a wolf's temperament. He didn't seem to have a fierce bone in his body. Nor did he look anything like a wolf. Breeding had given him ears that flopped limply down instead of standing up alertly. His curly black coat didn't shed the way a wolf's did. Instead, he needed regular haircuts. If, by some accident, Pete became feral, his hair would just keep growing until it reached to the ground like a yak's.

Pete seemed far, far removed from his wolfish origins.

There was something a little sad about that. Lorenz wrote that he preferred chows and German shepherd dogs because of their wolfishness. He said he felt more honored by the friendship of an animal closer to the wild prototype. He complained of the "promiscuous friendliness" of dogs like Pete. It was true. Pete seemed to love everyone.

I found myself wishing that Pete would show his wolfish side a little. Maybe it was just his environment, I thought. After all, living in a comfortable house in a suburb wasn't particularly conducive to hearing the call of the wild.

One summer, we went camping in the Adirondacks. We slept in tents, cooked over an open fire, ate sitting on the ground, and used a Coleman lantern for light. During the day we rowed out to a little rocky island where we all went swimming. Pete loved the water and was soon jumping from a pointy rock that hung out over the water. Once he started, there was no stopping him. We have a framed photo of him in the middle of one of those leaps. He looks like a flying dog.

After dinner I walked to the edge of our site and peered into the darkness. Beyond our ring of light, I knew, were raccoons, skunks, porcupine, rabbits, chipmunks, field mice, deer, lynx, coyotes, and bear. Pete could probably smell and hear their presence. Would he hear the call of the wild? Would he be drawn to something out there, like the dogs in the Jack London stories? Would he pull away from us a bit, try to wander off into the woods?

"Pete wants a walk," said Janet.

I turned to see Pete standing there. He was giving me that look, the one that said, *When are we going out?*

"Pete," I said. "We're already outside. You don't need me to go for a walk."

He just kept staring at me. The children were both laughing. Janet handed me a flashlight.

"Creature of habit," she said.

I felt ridiculous, but I gave in.

"Okay, come on, Pete," I said.

He bounded along next to me.

We started on the path away from the campground area. The woods got thicker and darker. Pete, I noticed, was walking behind me, the way he did when we used to go into the dark alley. He was no Lupo.

I turned on my flashlight. It shown brightly for a few seconds, then went dim. I remembered that I had given the children the job of making sure that all the flashlights had fresh batteries.

I stopped walking, hoping that Pete would take the hint and go. "Come on, Pete," I said.

Finally, I heard him rustling in the leaves in that slightly hasty way that precedes a squat. And as if in recognition of the event, there was a loud hoot. Then another. I'd never heard an owl in the wild, but I knew immediately that's what it was. It sounded very close. I shined my weak light in the direction of the sound. I picked up the white wood of a dead tree and followed it up. There, on the broken-off splintered top of the tree was the owl. He hooted once more and flew off on silent wings.

When I looked around for Pete, he was already turned toward the camp. He had heard the call of the wild, but was going in the opposite direction.

When we got back, I told everyone about the owl.

"We heard it," said Janet. "You weren't that far away."

"I saw its yellow eyes," I said.

The children were imitating the owl's cry, directing their hoots out into the darkness.

"That's not how you lure an owl," I said, remembering something that a park ranger had once shown me. "You make your hand go like this," I said, demonstrating how, by making a fist and then loudly kissing the mouth-like place where thumb and finger curl together, you could make a squeaking sound.

"That sounds like a mouse to them and they'll swoop down to grab it," I said.

Janet looked at me. "Oh, good idea, owls diving down at the children."

"Well, they don't actually follow through," I said. "They're just supposed to come to have a look."

The kids were squeaking their hands like mad and competing to make the loudest squeak. But the owl, if it was still around, wasn't fooled.

Later I helped the children spread out their sleeping bags inside their tent. When I crawled out, Pete was staring at me, again.

"What, another walk?" I said.

"He wants to get in the tent," said Alex.

I had imagined—in my *Call of the Wild* scenario—that Pete would sleep outside our flimsy shelters, like a Stone Age guardian. I had pictured him as our buffer with the wild world. Now, here he was pulling a long face because he was being left outside.

"Pete can sleep with us," said Claire.

"Can he fit?" I asked.

"There's room in the middle," said Alex, who was already in his bag and scrunching himself over to one side of the tent.

So Pete went in with the kids.

Lying on my back in the pitch-black interior of the tent, I listened to the frogs croaking loudly down by the lake. I thought about the owl, and the wolf diorama, and this whole business about Pete and his alleged wild side. It was silly, I realized. If Pete were truly wild, he'd be like one of those troublesome dogs that kills cats or isn't safe around people.

Lastly, who was I to broadcast all these regrets about wildness lost? I certainly wasn't wild. Not only was I ill-suited to survive in the wilderness, I wasn't even wild in the social sense. Not since we moved out of the loft in the city. Like Pete, I had heeded the call of the mild.

CHAPTER ELEVEN

Life in the Woods

Wolves in the wild spend several hours a day walking their territory. Homeless village dogs and roaming rural dogs do the same thing. The wolves have vast territories, from 20 to 500 square miles. The dogs' territories are much smaller—sometimes less than a mile, but the patterns are the same.

People are sometimes puzzled by these activities because they expect animals to be pursuing something specific, like food or sex. But these roaming canids are not necessarily hunting or scavenging for food. Nor are they searching for mates. Nor guarding the borders of their territory (they spend most of their time on the interior paths and crossroads). Of course, these excursions could involve any of these things—hunting, mating, fighting, socializing. But what the wolves and the free-range dogs are mostly doing is *reconnoitering*. They're looking around, checking up on things. They're gathering information. They're observing the tracks and scat of other animals. They're observing changes in the landscape: a fallen tree, a stream that's flooded its banks, the remains of a fire. They're sniffing at scent markings left by other members of their species, and leaving their own in response.

Paleolithic humans, our primitive forebears, led daily lives that closely paralleled those of wolves. As hunter-gatherers, they had similar habits (minus the scent marking). Before humans farmed and kept domestic animals, they, too, went out reconnoitering. As with the wolves, the key to survival was in knowing the land: the location of water, what plants were edible, the habits and dwelling places of animals, the seasonal cycles. Like the wolves, they went out to forage and hunt, but also simply to observe, investigate, and explore.

In time, the little "Mystery Trails" nature area became our woods. No one—besides the few animals that lived there—reconnoitered there as much as Pete and I did. We went every day, sometimes twice a day, in every season in every kind of weather.

When we met people, I secretly tested their knowledge of the place: "Did you notice all the branches that came down in the ice storm?" "Does it bother you that the kids have been partying a lot . . . ?" "Have you seen the woodpecker? . . . the pet rabbit? . . . the wild turkey? . . . the stolen motorcycle?"

And when they said, "Really?" or "No, I hadn't noticed," or "I didn't know turkeys lived around here," I was pleased, and felt confirmed in my conviction that this was our territory.

I loved that feeling of walking in, of passing from the neighborhood of houses and streets and cars into the woods. A forest wasn't like a park or an arboretum, where the trees were elements in a larger environment. Here the trees *were* the environment. It was an enclosed world, like a cathedral, except that the walls, the ceiling, and the structural supports were all alive. Trees leaned in from either side of the broad central aisle to form a lofty arch. Sunlight pierced the foliage and beamed down like the light from a clerestory window.

Trees were responsible for the crunchy, leafy floor of the place. They determined which plants could live beneath them. They screened out the neighborhood noise and substituted their own soundtrack of creaking branches, rustling foliage, scrambling squirrels, and pecking woodpeckers. Their growth and their rot gave the place its smell, their bark and foliage its color.

The main trail became so familiar to me that I could walk it on moonless nights without tripping on a root or declivity.

Occasionally an entire elementary school class came traipsing through like a line of elves. Pete would encounter them ahead on the trail and I'd hear their little shrieks as he moved down their line.

About once a week, we'd run into sweet old George Thompson and his two dogs, Brindle and Mops. George was a lifelong resident of town. He was a retired teacher, about seventy-five, with watery blue eyes and a droopy moustache yellowed by tobacco smoke. He wore baggy sweaters, a tweedy golf hat, and a many-buckled trench coat.

Mops, the smaller dog, looked like a slipper that had been through the washing machine. Brindle was a wolfish collie with half of a tongue. Years ago, she'd been hit by a car. Every now and then, George told me the story of the accident, which he always ended by prying open Brindle's mouth to show me the missing teeth and the sliver-shaped tongue.

George wasn't much of a walker. Once he was a few steps into the woods and had released the dogs, he'd get down to what for him was the true pleasure of dog walking: serious smoking. His wife wouldn't let him smoke in the house, so he had to cram all of it into these walks. He'd start with a pipe, puff thoughtfully on that for a while, switch to a filtered cigarette, smoke that down, pause a minute or two, then get out the pipe again.

Brindle had the shepherd dog's compulsion to herd. Let off the leash, she'd run with Pete for about ten or fifteen yards, and then—her anxiety taking hold—she'd herd him back to us again. She couldn't rest easy unless all the living things around her were in a tight little group.

George had been a high school football star. "I know I don't look it now," he'd say, "but I was big back then. Two hundred twenty pounds."

He was like a boy who couldn't quite believe he had grown up, much less grown old. "You'll see," he was always saying to me, when reminded of where time had deposited him.

What I liked about George was the easy rapport he had with his dogs. He didn't hold himself too high above his animals. He treated them almost like equals. In this sense, he was a bit of a rustic, like Eumaeus, the loyal swineherd, who looked after Odysseus's dog, Argos, during his fourteen-year absence.

After ten minutes or so with George, I'd start shifting from foot to foot, not wanting to be impolite, but eager to get walking.

"Oh sure, go ahead, go ahead," he'd say, gesturing with his pipe or cigarette but looking disappointed all the same.

Most of the time it was just Pete and me.

Sometimes, a big wind would topple a tree and we'd arrive to see the aftermath: the ripped-up root ball and the raw earthen crater in the fern-carpeted floor. Other trees died more gradual deaths. One would fall a bit, then come to rest up against the others like a drunk supported by friends. Sometimes one would grow for a while in that position, tilted at an odd 45-degree angle until gravity finished it off.

Outside, it was Eastern Standard or Daylight Savings Time.

Inside, it was Forest Time.

When Pete found a raccoon carcass, its decomposition became a calendar-clock. Every day, there was less of it. The sun worked on it from the top, the insects and maggots from underneath. At night, mice gnawed on the teeth and bones and plucked fur to line their nests. Eventually there was only a flat leathery skin. That remained a long time, but gradually blended into the earth so that you had to poke around to find it beneath the leaves.

Another clock was that spot where the kids had chopped down trees. I watched the forest recover from the wound. First, the crowns of the neighboring trees leaned in to grab additional light. Meanwhile, some of the truncated victims proved only stunned. When spring came, they sprouted suckers, and lateral branches that curved up, aspiring to be new trunks. This image—of a stump sprouting new growth—was a popular symbol in Renaissance paintings. Artists used it in paintings of Christ's birth or New Testament episodes like *The Flight into Egypt*. The severed trunk foretold the crucifixion and the sprouting stump the resurrection.

Trees may be mute, and stationary, and helpless to fend off attacks from boys with axes, but they have a trick or two of their own. One of them is this: You can cut them off at a height even with your shoe tops, and some of them will grow back. I watched for about five years. While Pete and I aged, these damaged trees were having a second life, although it didn't look as if they'd ever regain their former stature. Some sent out so many suckers that they seemed headed for new destinies as bushes.

Forest time slowed to a crawl in the winter. The trees held their breath, became as inert as rocks. In spring, they'd silently swell with life. Sap would flow. They'd add another ring of cambium, push out buds, unfold new leaves. When millions of tiny changes happen at once, a forest can open like a page in a pop-up book.

Once sped up, it could seem out of control. One spring day, trailing behind galloping Pete, I saw every paw print on the trail's soft edge squirming with life. I bent over and stirred up inches of black crumbly soil. Pink worms were wriggling everywhere.

Forest Time could be deceptive, not just because of its stops and sudden accelerations, but because it was cyclical. Events repeated. The seasons swung around again. Growth and decay brought changes, but they canceled each other out. Evidence of a death was erased. New growth blended in anonymously with old. Most trees didn't look any older from one year to the next.

Outside, however, time moved in a straight line.

One day Pete and I came out of the forest and found the children transformed. Cherubic Claire had grown long, coltish legs and angular features. Alex, whose picture on the mantel showed a boy with tousled hair and pudgy, mud-spattered legs, had been replaced by a boy with slicked down cowlicks who was always punching his baseball mitt.

While Pete and I drifted along on Forest Time, five years had gone by.

Nor had we escaped. One day, pausing at the front door in the bright sunlight, I looked at Pete and noticed . . . gray hair. Could it be? He was still black, but not the lustrous black he had once been. He was peppered with gray.

We had spent five years daily traipsing through a little woods. It was hardly on par with Thoreau's complete immersion in Walden Woods—and yet . . . repetition makes scholars of us. It makes fishermen scholars of the sea, farmers scholars of the soil, and pilots scholars of the weather. All of us, if our lives are any good at all, become scholars of something.

It was a sweet time, but we'd outgrown it. There had been days when I felt trapped on a conveyor belt going round and round past "North American Forest" dioramas. How did prehistoric hunter-gatherers know when it was time to move on? Perhaps they saw game and food sources dwindling. Or they followed migrating herds. Or they retreated in the face of advancing ice. Maybe competing tribes drove them out. Maybe they just got restless. Maybe, like us, they just wanted more space.

CHAPTER TWELVE

Big Sky Country

But where to go? This was the suburbs, after all, not the edge of the frontier. One of my coworkers recommended a place she called "dog paradise." But it turned out to be a state forest preserve at the north end of the county. When she got to the part about a mountaintop pond "where all the dogs go swimming," I realized that I had been there.

It was too far and too big of a production for everyday dog walks. Besides, I hadn't even liked it. It was *too much* of a dog place. The people wore doggy first-aid kits and the dogs wore doggy backpacks. Decals on the cars advertised favored breeds: "I love my Lab" and "Airedale on Board." Mostly, though, it just had too many rules.

I got a better tip from a bicyclist friend who told me about a park in the adjacent town. "Hardly anyone uses it," he said.

The next day, I put Pete in the back of the Roadmaster station wagon—an old monster of a car that made a perfect dog-mobile— and drove the mile or so to the park. I could see why nobody used it. It was on the wrong side of the railroad tracks behind an industrial zone. Flanking its entrance was a ShopRite supermarket and the local cable company. Satellite dishes, aligned like sunflowers, pointed to the sky above the park.

The park, which fronted the Overpeck Creek, was called Over-peck South. Up creek, in my town, was Overpeck North. The two were separated by a wild and marshy area, which, for some reason, had never been made into a park.

The Overpeck looked too big to be a creek and in places it looked as wide as a lake. Both parks were plain and utilitarian, each a narrow string of hard-surface courts, playing fields, and running tracks. They had more in common with the nearby turnpike than with the natural creek. Right on the border of the wild area was the county horseback-riding center, tucked behind a screen of willow trees and oaks.

Overpeck North flanked a busy country road and was the better-maintained and more popular of the parks. Its great circle drew a semi-chaotic, but good-natured mix of runners, walkers, bicyclists, and roller skaters. Early on, I had taken Pete there. The spacious area inside the great circle looked like a perfect place to let a dog run free, but the park police made regular patrols in their bullhorn-equipped trucks. They picked us out easily on the tree-less landscape and issued amplified commands that resounded above our heads like the voice of God.

Overpeck South didn't give the impression of a place that would have vigilant police patrols. It was practically deserted. On that first day, I saw a sole jogger running along a cinder track. With Pete surveying the scene from the back of the station wagon, we drove the length of the park next to the creek. I took it in: old picnic tables, scruffy ball fields, bent backstops, rickety bleachers, sagging tennis nets, and windblown supermarket bags. It looked perfect. It offered us the standard fringe deal: In exchange for tolerating some aesthetic shortcomings, we'd be free. I signed on the dotted line, Pete made his mark, and the place was ours.

The town where I grew up, ordinary in most ways, had beautiful turn-of-the-century parks. They hugged two crisscrossing rivers that made a giant X on the town map. As a kid, I could get from one corner of town to the other without ever leaving the parks. These parks had all the usual recreation facilities, but they also had romantic *allees* of sycamore trees, stands of pines, ponds, groves, curving paths, and arching wooden bridges.

I didn't know it then, but these parks of my childhood probably owed their romantic landscaping to Frederick Law Olmsted. He didn't design them, but they were probably inspired by an older Olmsted park in the nearby central city. Olmsted was co-creator of Manhattan's Central Park and the towering giant of park design in this country. He laid out great parks all over North America—Chicago, Boston, Buffalo, Montreal—and influenced the design of countless others. Anyone who walks a dog in a park and feels a kind of poetry in the landscape probably has Olmsted to thank for it.

Olmsted, a contemporary of Thoreau, was born in Hartford, Connecticut, in 1822. He was another early-to-mid-nineteenth-century self-invented man who had a passion for nature. In his early career he alternated between farming on Staten Island

and journalism. In his late twenties, he traveled to England and, impressed by the public gardens and parks there, published *Walks and Talks of an American Farmer in England.*

In 1858 he and the English-born architect Calvert Vaux, who had previously collaborated with the influential landscape designer Andrew Jackson Downing, won the competition to design Central Park in Manhattan. Their "Greensward Plan" called for a park that would be organized around a sequence of greenswards, or meadows, a large-scale application of the "picturesque" aesthetic that Downing had made so popular. It was based on the same sort of picturesque settings that Downing had used for his house designs, a style that had its roots in Old Master landscapes. Olmsted and Vaux were quite forthright in their belief that a park should be a walk-in landscape painting, or what Olmsted called "passages of scenery."

Most people don't realize how artificial Central Park is. I used to think that the park's natural features were the aboriginal landscape of Manhattan peeking through. In truth, Central Park as a "place" is entirely designed. There is hardly a hill, a rock, a shoreline, a tree, or a bush that wasn't put there for artistic effect. Thousands of workers labored for more than fifteen years on its construction. They filled holes, blasted rock, excavated lakes, moved millions of cubic yards of soil, installed a vast network of subterranean water and drainage pipes, and planted an estimated four to five million trees, shrubs, and vines.

Olmsted's approach wasn't popular with everyone. Many politicians and reformers of the time believed a park for common citizens should provide less poetry and more swimming pools and playing fields.

But Olmsted's and Vaux's vision prevailed. The park was constructed as a place for repose and contemplative pleasures (though some ball fields and basketball courts were added later). Today the pendulum of park design has swung back to the recreational.

All this matters quite a bit to dog walkers, who flock to parks in greater and greater numbers and who, unlike the strenuously engaged softball players, roller bladers, bicyclists, runners, and Frisbee throwers, approach the place in the receptive mood that Olmsted probably envisioned. They and their dogs are there for the naturalism, and if part of their inspired response has been to set their dogs loose, beleaguered parks administrators can put some of the blame on the man who made the park.

Like Central Park, my park had a meadow, but unlike Olmsted's carefully composed meadows, mine didn't seem planned at all. It appeared to exist only because the L-shaped road that ran through the park cut off a piece of land that wasn't big enough or level enough for a baseball or soccer field. It was an accidental meadow.

Soon I was pulling into the little parking area, opening the back of the station wagon, and with a quick look around for the park patrol, setting Pete free. He would be off in a flash—full throttle. He didn't need sticks or Frisbees to get him running. He ran because that's what a meadow invited him to do.

And when he ran, half of me went with him. There's something about a dog racing across a great expanse that can make your heart soar. I strode after him, conscious of the miles of sky above my head, the rolling ground beneath my feet. I watched Pete open up the distance between us until I could cover his black shape with the fingernail on my extended pinky. He ended with a flourish, pulling up on stiffened legs into a question-mark curve that seemed to ask: *"What's taking you so long?"*

We were sometimes joined by golfers hitting chip shots out of the dips, or a Tai Chi practitioner standing statue-like on one of the rises. In the summer, sunbathers relied on its spaciousness for privacy. Sometimes the park police cruised through and yelled at me. But nineteen out of twenty times we were in sole possession, as apart from human society as a shepherd and his sheepdog.

Countless artists, I now realized, had played to this natural human affinity for meadows. The Old Masters peopled theirs with frolicking nymphs and satyrs. Monet and Renoir dropped mothers and children into lush poppy fields. Winslow Homer set loose boys to play "snap the whip." John Constable, Jean-Baptiste-Camille Corot, Claude Lorraine, and George Inness—the list went on and on. Meadows are so consistently rendered by artists as sweet, friendly places that Andrew Wyeth's agoraphobic *Christina's World,* in which a crippled girl is stranded in a field, stands out as a strange anomaly.

There was one other feature of this park that seemed intentionally poetic: a bow-shaped grove of catalpa trees and a single pine. I found this place charming, despite its location along the chain-link fence of the supermarket parking lot. The other side was bordered by a line of tall, fan-shaped privet bushes that blossomed with an intoxicating fragrance in May.

Just eighty or so yards long and maybe half as wide, the Grove sat next to the park's entrance like a coat closet at the front door. Its northern catalpas put on a four-season show: They flowered in the spring, grew green crescent-shaped seed pods in the summer, dropped the then-purplish pods in the fall, and threw up irregular, zigzagging branches against the winter sky. The pine had long ago lost its top to storms or heavy snow and stood, gnarled and asymmetrical, like the windblown trees in Chinese paintings.

Several woodchucks led happy existences there. At twilight, when the tree trunks darkened and the grass turned a deeper green, rabbits loped in to graze. I framed it up as a painting many times and showed it off to friends as proof of the beauty in unexpected places that dog walking offered.

In the winter, flocks—*gaggles*—of Canada geese descended on our meadow. On rainy days there might be 300 of them nibbling on the soggy turf. They were handsome black-and-white birds, but they left acres of green poop wherever they grazed. Chasing them seemed a public service.

In charging them, Pete never had a chance—or probably any intention—of catching one. To do so would have required stealth and timing, and he had neither. The geese were almost as inept, however, which at least gave the appearance of a contest.

The birds honked nervously when we approached and fell into formation, every bird in profile, one eye staring, like birds in an Egyptian relief. For reasons I never understood, Pete always charged toward a point behind the flock. Maybe that was his idea of a ruse. It did seem to confuse the geese a little. The first honks were low, like a murmur. They debated the threat as if hoping that this four-legged creature had some other target in mind.

As Pete straightened out his trajectory, they sounded the Mayday alert. The ones in the front took off first so that they rose in a wave. They were heavy birds, slow to get off the ground. They stood upright for takeoff, hundreds of wings pumping with a sound like a huge sheet of canvas flapping in a gale.

As Pete caught up, the ones in the back might only be three or four feet off the ground. A hungry wolf might have made a desperate leap, but Pete, neither wolf nor hungry, was already going into his victory lap. Filling the sky with so many honking geese went to his head, I think. I couldn't blame him. It was a thrilling sight.

Then it was time for a drink. Pete would find a break in the bushes and disappear down a gully. I'd follow, ducking and grabbing twisty trunks for support.

Pete was always ankle deep and noisily lapping when I arrived. He drank with such noisy pleasure that I felt like I was having a drink myself. Sometimes the geese he'd scattered were floating offshore, honking nervously at their tormenter's reappearance. Sometimes there were black diving birds with snakelike necks. Or a wading egret in an adjacent cove. Sometimes a log drifted by in the current, its branches rising and falling like the arms of a drowning man.

But we hung around, regardless. The creek was always worth looking at. Izaak Walton's *The Compleat Angler*, written in 1653, contains the quote: "Rivers and the inhabitants of the watery element were made for wise men to contemplate, and fools to pass by without consideration."

I can't say whether I was wise for wanting to stand there and look, but if I was, Pete was, as well. He was right there, with one of those doggy smiles on his face.

CHAPTER THIRTEEN

Dog-walking Society

Dogs are social lubricators. Most are so absurdly friendly as to make even shy or misanthropic companions seem gregarious. They will literally drag you in the direction of another dog and its walker—just as your mother once did, saying: *"Here is a little friend for you! Don't be shy!"*

Once you are within a leash-length of the other dog walker, your dog will demonstrate the proper greeting for a new acquaintance: effusive butt licking, groin sniffing, and spirited humping. Those who aren't embarrassed by these excesses may come to appreciate it as a feature of dog-walking life. Dogs provide a way of meeting new people without any of the usual formalities or potential for rejection. It's no secret that single people in cities get dogs as a way of meeting other singles. They smile or shrug as Bowser or Charlie pulls them toward a stranger of the opposite sex. *"What can I do? He's so damn friendly!"*

Paired up with a dog, you become a new social entity, a two-headed creature.

Richard, fellow dupe from the neighborhood, was a sensitive, intelligent man, but the cloud of confusion that Jambo threw up turned him into a temporarily ridiculous figure.

Pete, on the other hand, was so universally admired that I sometimes felt more socially desirable with him, than on my own.

A woman whose dog would regularly beat up Pete in the woods may have been a nice person, but it was hard for me to see this when her canine half had its jaws clamped on the throat of mine.

Over the years, I have learned to read the characters of various dog-walking pairs. There were those who wanted nothing to do with us: the people who crossed to the other side of the street when they saw us coming. Or, worse, the ones we sometimes encountered in the woods who, upon seeing Pete off the leash, would yell and wave in a panic before the human half gathered up the dog half (usually a fluffy white lap dog) and stormed angrily away.

More often, the dogs' intense interest in each other wins out. Because of this, the dog-walking world is friendlier than the regular world. If you have a nice dog and the other person has a nice dog, and the two dogs are pulling together like magnets, the feeling of openness and goodwill is contagious. You want to be as unconditional and unequivocal with people as your dog is with other dogs.

This can have its pitfalls. Once, in an effort to be a friendlier, more doglike human, I became entangled in the equivalent of a dog-walking marriage.

This happened back in the woods. Bill Pemberton was a fellow parent. We met on the open-school-night-Christmas-concert-parent-teacher-bake-sale circuit. He was a tall, ruddy man with eyes that turned to merry slits when he smiled. At a party one night, I got onto the subject of dog walking. I suppose I waxed a bit too enthusiastically about Thoreau, the mysteries of the forest, the shadow people—all of it. Without realizing it, I converted him.

A few days later, he and his black Lab-mix, Molly, showed up on the Mystery Trails. Molly had a barrel-shaped body on sticklike legs. She and Pete romped, wrestled, and played keep-away. They raced down trails and drank noisily from the tiny stream. They even attempted a little sex. Molly was spayed, but it didn't matter, because neither dog seemed able to align the proper parts. Pete would thrust in the direction of Molly's head. Molly would hump Pete's shoulder. Mostly they just drooled on each other. Watching them, I wondered how dogs ever reproduced.

Bill's idea of a good walk was one that exhausted Molly. "That's what I like to see, Molly," he'd say when his dog's tongue was dangling four or five inches from her mouth.

In the beginning, we'd run into them about twice a week. Sometimes, however, one pair would be leaving when the other was arriving, which always disappointed the dogs. This led Bill to pop the question.

"Why don't we walk our dogs together?" he said one day.

An alarm went off in my head. I hemmed and hawed. What about the opportunities to clear my mind, to have a Thoreau-like solitude in communion with nature? Besides, I hardly knew him.

But it was hard to say no to Bill Pemberton. He was, himself, like a big friendly dog. He beamed and nodded with the human equivalents of tail wags and face licks. He was so open and friendly, projected such goodwill and optimism, that I would have felt like a Grinch saying no.

I mumbled something about "trying it out."

The knot was tied.

Soon, because it was more convenient that way (Bill's wife took the family's only car to work), I was picking up Bill and Molly on my way back from dropping Claire at the middle school and driving us all up to the woods. And driving Bill and Molly back.

Bill, I should mention, was a Protestant minister. This, admittedly, made me a little self-conscious. I was never quite sure what was appropriate and inappropriate to say to him. I knew better than to admit to coveting my neighbor's wife, but could I describe one of the baseball-team mothers as "hot." More to the point, in saying such a thing, was I *confessing* rather than simply talking with another guy? And, when you got right down to it, wasn't it his ministerial duty to convert me?

His being a minister wasn't the real problem, however. The real problem was the sheer amount of time we spent together: a good forty-five minutes a day, six days a week (fortunately, he had to preach on Sunday).

That's a lot of time to spend talking with anyone. It's the amount of time people devote—or used to devote—to intense psychoanalysis. There were days when I spent more time in conversation with Bill than with my wife.

The relationship really couldn't sustain all this. After about eight months, it felt like pure duty. I was thinking up excuses for skipping a day. These became more numerous, but the relationship dragged on and endured for another two months. We were staying together for the sake of the dogs.

Dog Walks Man

Finally, I told Bill that I was writing a book (not entirely untrue) and that, as much as I would miss him, the half hour of solitude in the morning was essential to the process. He took it well.

Soon Pete and I were on our own again. I varied my schedule to avoid running into Bill, but it sometimes happened. The dogs would have a happy reunion, while Bill and I shifted from foot to foot and smiled awkwardly at each other, just like two exes.

Few dog-walking acquaintanceships turned this sticky. In fact, most were more socially circumscribed than other casual relationships. This was especially true if the two people were of the opposite sex. Perhaps it was a counterbalance to the randy behavior that the dogs brought to the encounter, but I always became extremely polite in these conversations. The two dogs might have quickly advanced to oral-genital contact, but I'd be as proper as a gentleman in a Jane Austen novel.

Another unspoken rule was that these conversations should focus on the dogs. You could talk about vets and breeders, how and when you each got your dogs, dog quirks and ailments, skunk encounters, mailman relations, problem behaviors, and defecation habits. There was nothing too intimate to be shared about the dogs. You might learn, for example, that a dog named Ruffie had a bad habit of humping visitors' legs. You might furthermore learn that, because of this problem, poor Ruffie already had a vet appointment for castration. Meanwhile, you still wouldn't even know the name of Ruffie's owner.

How many times, in relating a story to Janet had I referred to another dog walker as "Ruffie's owner," or even "Ruffie's mother"? Other times, I made up nicknames for people.

So it was with a woman dog walker I came to call Cassandra (after the prophet of doom in *The Trojan War*). We met Cassandra and her two small mixed-breed dogs at the periphery of our meadow. Cassandra never let her dogs off leash, so the meadow didn't mean anything special to her. She made one big circuit around the perimeter of the park. This took her along the edge of the meadow, next to the creek, around the three ball fields and the running track, past the tennis courts and along the cable company fence. She did one circuit without pausing and then walked right out the gate without breaking stride. That was her style: once around and out. Of course, our dogs would start socializing. And, since she never let hers go, or stopped walking, I'd end up tagging along. She had a British accent and was some kind of scientist—a chemist or a biologist, I think.

One day, when Pete stopped to drink from a puddle, she shook her head in dismay.

"You shouldn't let him do that," she said.

I asked why.

"He can get *leptospirosis*," she said.

I knew nothing about leptospirosis but didn't want to appear totally ignorant, so I said I didn't know they could get it from puddle water.

"The parasite thrives in puddles," she said.

Was it serious?

"It can be fatal," she said.

Pete was behind us now, still lapping away at the puddle.

"And communicable to humans," she added.

"C'mon, Pete," I said. "That's enough."

What was I supposed to do? Put my dog on a short lead and drag him away from every puddle we encountered? What about his dashes across the meadow? The routing of the geese? The immersions in the creek? I'd never even heard of a dog getting this illness.

A week later, she was warning me about another puddle-borne disease, *giardiasis*. She said she knew someone in Vermont who had contracted it from her basset hound.

"She lost thirty-six pounds before it was correctly diagnosed."

She reminded me of those new parents in town who didn't let their children walk to school, who suspected that kidnappers and perverts were always lurking about, that Halloween candy was probably poisoned, and that most playground equipment was designed to cause spinal-cord injuries.

When Pete chased a groundhog one day, she shook her head ominously.

I assured her that the groundhog was in no danger.

"It's the dog you have to worry about, not the groundhog," she said.

"Do they bite?" I asked.

"The groundhog flips onto its back and claws upwards," Cassandra said, making a claw out of three fingers and scratching at the air. "Their nails are razor-sharp. They can eviscerate a dog."

Where did she get these things? Even her language. Not "injure" or "wound," but *eviscerate.*

I knew it was only a matter of time before she brought up Lyme disease.

This time, at least, I was informed.

The Great Lyme Disease Scare of the 1990s swept the Northeast when Claire and Alex were small. It created a wave of parental paranoia that hadn't been seen since the polio epidemic of my own childhood.

We vacationed with family at the Connecticut shore, where the scourge was first identified, so we were continually exposed to warnings posted at beach bathhouses and on hiking trails. In subsequent vacation spots, the disease seemed to have followed us: Sandy Hook, Block Island, Martha's Vineyard. Magazines ran cover stories on it.

The tiny deer tick that spread the disease was always described in news stories and doctor's office pamphlets as being "the size of the period at the end of this sentence," no matter what size typeface the story was printed in.

Parents were told to dress their children in light-colored clothing and to inspect their bodies nightly for the miniscule tick. Every night we scanned arms, legs, backs, stomachs, hair, and backs of knees for ticks. We watched for the dreaded bull's-eye rash.

Cassandra saw her opening when Pete went poking around in the reeds at the edge of the Meadowlands.

"He'll pick up ticks in there," she said. "Lyme disease, you know."

"He's only got one foot in," I said.

She said nothing.

"There aren't any deer around here," I said.

She shook her head. *Oh, the stupidity of mankind.* "The primary carriers are white-footed mice."

Soon she was narrating a tale that could have been written by Stephen King.

The victim was a distant relative in her husband's family, a second cousin's son or something. But she knew every detail. The boy was eight or nine. The family lived in one of those exurbs where the backyards were frequently visited by deer and bears. No one had detected the disease in the early stages.

Soon the boy had "mysterious fatigue and heart palpitations." As she warmed to her story, a cold wind blew in off the creek. "The disease went undetected into the advanced and untreatable stages," she said. "By the time they figured out what it was, it was beyond the reach of the antibiotics." I listened in respectful silence. "His legs became so weak and arthritic that his father had to carry him up to bed every night."

Later I remarked that our veterinarian had given us a repellant for ticks. It was a potent green gel that you squeezed between the dog's shoulder blades. Everyone swore by it. You only had to apply it once every few months during the season to control the ticks.

For once Cassandra agreed with me. "It works," she said. Then added, "Too well."

I waited.

"The ticks jump off the dogs and onto you," she said. "At least the other way I know where they are."

Checkmated, again.

After I met Cassandra, I kept coming across stories about dog-walking tragedies. Out of Florida came the one about an eighty-one-year-old dog walker who was attacked by an alligator. It dragged him into the water and bit off his leg. The man died of fright, or blood loss, or both.

Then there was the Manhattan woman who was electrocuted on a slushy sidewalk while walking two dogs in the East Village. Current had leaked from corroded wires and through a metal plate that she and her dogs were standing on. The dogs were uninjured.

Danger lurked even in Central Park's picturesque boating lake, where a Jack Russell terrier was set upon by a swan. The bird hit the dog with its powerful wings, then, as reported in the *New York Post*, "beaked his head again and again" until it drowned.

Inspired by Cassandra, I now have a collection of such stories from the Internet. They tell of dogs and their walkers hit by cars, struck by lightning, bitten by snakes, mauled by raccoons, spiked by porcupines, and shot by hunters. One of the most frequent dog-walking tragedies occurs when dogs run out onto frozen lakes or ponds, fall through the ice, can't get up out of the hole, and draw well-intentioned owners to the same fate.

Jack London's famous short story "To Build a Fire" can be read as a dog-walking tragedy in one act. A man and his dog set out on the Yukon Trail in temperatures that are seventy below zero. The man gets his boots wet and desperately needs to make a fire to dry them, but things keep going wrong. He drops the matches. Some falling snow douses the fire. Finally he is out of matches. His feet freeze, followed by the rest of him. The dog, who had known all along that this was a bad idea, lopes back to the outpost.

As shocking as they were, such stories provided me with a previously missing element in the dog-walking experience: a feeling of danger and suspense.

"Who knows what might happen to us," I'd say to Pete, as we set out on what I imagined newspaper writers would later portentously write, *"had seemed like an ordinary dog walk . . ."*

CHAPTER FOURTEEN

Forbidden Forest

Cassandra's mirror opposite was a dog walker named Joe. Joe didn't worry about anything, or at least anything in the natural world. He was a big guy with a scraggly white beard, long hair that stuck out the bottom of his hunter's cap, and spidery red lines across his nose.

He was always just "Joe." I never learned his last name. His dog, a yellow Lab, was "Mike." Whenever I pulled into the parking lot of Overpeck South, and saw the two of them standing near the small camper truck, I'd have a moment of doubt as to which one was which.

Joe would puff on his pipe and give me the standard New Jersey greeting: "How ya doin'?" Then Mike and Pete would take off across the meadow and Joe and I would talk in the parking lot.

Joe was one of those outdoorsmen who get stir-crazy if they're indoors for too many hours. He frequently went away on hunting and fishing trips, but when he was home, he came to the park three or four times a day. He craved the outdoors, even though he couldn't move around in it much once he got there. An injury in Vietnam had left him with a bad hitch in his walk. He had figured out ways to hunt and fish from mostly stationary positions and, when out with his dog, never strayed far from his car. So it was always easy to find him. He was either in the little parking lot or the Grove. Joe belonged to a hunter-and-fisherman group centered on the Hudson River and knew a lot about the animals and plants around us. From him I learned that the creek had carp, catfish, largemouth bass, eels, and sunfish, but that it wasn't safe to eat any of them because the tidal waters from Newark Bay came up this far. I found out that the ducks I'd seen with disk-shaped heads were called mergansers and that the diving birds I called loons were actually cormorants. He pointed out red-tailed hawks, northern harriers, and ospreys. He said he'd seen snapping turtles come up into the meadow to lay their eggs.

One day, watching Pete and Mike chase a groundhog, I mentioned Cassandra's warnings about the raking claws.

"Could happen," he said with a shrug. "But I've never seen it."

I told him about a passage in *Walden* where Thoreau, angered after a woodchuck had ravaged his bean garden, killed the animal with a shovel, then ate it. This story surprises most people because of Thoreau's reputation for non-violence. But Joe had a different take.

"How did he cook it?" he wanted to know.

"I don't know," I said. "Why?"

"I've eaten woodchuck," he said. "You have to know how to prepare it."

"I think Thoreau said it was tough," I said.

He nodded, then launched into this bizarre hunter's recipe. The meat was cooked into submission by first boiling, then baking, then frying it. There were lots of coatings and sauces, too. He said he learned it from a very old Shoshone Indian who claimed to have fought with Mexican revolutionary Pancho Villa in 1916. When Joe met him he was in his eighties and living on Owassa Lake in New Jersey. The old Indian led a hunter-gatherer's life in late-twentieth-century New Jersey. He ate wild game and picked native plants. He reached the age of one hundred, Joe said.

The connection to this old Indian seemed to confirm my sense that Joe belonged to a surviving lineage of frontiersmen.

One evening in early November, Joe and I were standing in the tiny parking lot when a sound like a buzz saw came from beyond the thick wall of reeds at the edge of the meadow. It changed pitch as it receded and approached.

"Trail bikes," Joe said.

This surprised me. I told Joe I thought it was all swamp and thick growth in there.

"Nah," said Joe. "There's dry land. There's a dirt road that runs along next to the railroad tracks."

In fact, there was a path going in there at the back of the Grove, but I had never ventured in.

"What about the ticks?" I asked, recalling Cassandra.

"Too cold, now," said Joe.

The trail-bike buzz grew louder.

Of course, my reasons for not having explored this wild, unimproved area went beyond swampy terrain and ticks.

Where I lived, it was the *Forbidden Forest*.

In fairy tales, terrible fates befell those who entered the Forbidden Forest. These foolish souls were corrupted by devils, enslaved by witches, deceived by talking animals, scared witless by ghosts, crushed by giants, swallowed up by bubbling fire pits, or grabbed by the scraggly branches of trees.

In our enlightened world, the Forbidden Forest survived in a different form—the environmental hazard. Unlike the old myths, these were legitimate horrors, but they occupied the same psychic space as their fantastic predecessors. For witches and fire pits, substitute toxic dumps, radon-contaminated soil, Leukemia-inducing chemical canals.

My town had just such a place.

The Meadowlands.

Strangely, I passed it all the time. It was the wild and marshy zone between the two parks, a tract of about 120 acres—the size of an average eighteen-hole golf course. The tract was separated from the rest of the town by railroad tracks, a canal, fences, barriers, and keep-out signs.

It was there every time I drove down the steep hill to the local pool or the baseball fields. From that angle, you could look right down into its vast basin of tawny, undulating reeds. And yet, I ignored it. More than that, I didn't really see it. None of us did.

An aura of danger and degeneracy clung to this piece of land like radioactive contamination. Who knew where any of the rumors came from? They just seeped into people's minds: *The place was infested with rats. AIDS-infected hypodermic needles poked up out of the ground. Drug dealers and sex perverts called it home.*

But for the most part nobody talked about it. To virtuous eyes, it was invisible. It simply wasn't there.

The Forbidden Forest!

The Meadowlands!

As it turned out, our first expedition into the Meadowlands was launched not from the back of the Grove but from an entry point within my own town. A local teenager told me of a secret passage—a path and a plank—behind the town pool's parking lot. This so intrigued me that the very next morning, I put Pete in the back of the station wagon and pointed it in the direction of the pool. "We're going to the Meadowlands, Pete," I said, looking at him in the rearview mirror. "The Meadowlands." His floppy ears hitched up a notch and he smiled gamely. It was silly to be repeating it like that, but I was excited about the prospect of an adventure. The sixth or seventh time I said it, he woofed in annoyance.

This was in March, which meant the pool itself was closed. The gate was kept open for municipal trucks because at the back of the gravel parking lot was an area where the Public Works Department dumped snow, wood chips, and other debris. Beyond that was located an overgrown area and, sure enough, a path. After Pete sniffed and peed on a few of the tree stumps in the DPW area, we followed the path for about twenty yards until we came to a shallow drainage ditch. Someone had rolled a big barrel-shaped piece of concrete culvert into the ditch. The culvert made a steeply arched bridge. We climbed over that, went up and over the railroad bed, then came to a wider drainage canal. It was like an obstacle course. And yes, there was a nice broad plank. While Pete watched, I tested the plank's steadiness, then walked across, arms outstretched like a tightrope walker. On the other side, I called to him. "Come on, Pete," I said. He was wary. He nervously paced the bank, looking down at the water (which looked deep), at the wood (which he didn't trust), and at the air-travel distance (too far for a transcendent leap). He couldn't make up his mind.

It can be funny watching a dog trying to solve a problem like this, especially one like mine who thought about things to the point of neurotic indecision. "Come on, Pete," I said, hoping my excitement would catapult him across the canal. "The Meadowlands! The Meadowlands!" He whimpered in frustration and raced back and forth on the bank. "This way, Pete," I said, touching the plank with my foot. Finally, he put a tentative paw down on the wood, took one step forward, then, feeling the springiness, changed strategy and tried to leap the rest of the way. It wasn't a clean landing. His front legs cleared the crest of the bank, but his back legs landed in the water. He scrambled up to join me.

I patted him on the head. Barring any more obstacles, we had made it.

"Pete," I said. "We're in."

He woofed back at me.

Here was the road running parallel to the railroad tracks that Joe had described, and another road that branched off into the interior. Pete trotted around and sniffed the ground. I decided to explore the main road first. Pete and I walked south, a route that,

I later confirmed, led to the opening I'd seen at the back of the Grove.

For long stretches of this road, fifteen-foot-high reeds leaned in from both sides. A strange feeling came over me. We'd traveled only a few hundred yards and yet, it felt like we'd jumped continents. It was eerily quiet, except for the ever-present hum of the turnpike.

We walked for a while, and when the path proved unchanging, we doubled back to try a different direction. Back at the crossroads, we took the interior road. It was mid-morning. The sun was low in the sky but seemed stronger out here, like a tropical sun. A hawk wheeled in the bright blue sky. The road crossed a sluggish canal, its surface clotted with algae and duckweed. A half-dozen turtles flopped off their log. Beauty vied with desolation at every turn.

Soon we arrived at a plateau of chiseled boulders, rock that had been blasted out of some construction project years ago and dumped here. Ailanthus trees grew out of the crevices between the boulders. A few homely mullein plants with spiky yellow heads stood gathered in a group like hosts.

We were at the highest point in the area. The view opened up. It could have been the Everglades or the Serengeti Plains. Behind us was the rise leading up to the Palisades, on the slopes of which ran the tree-lined streets of my town. To the west was the creek. To the north and south, the Meadowlands stretched out expansively, its river of grasses stopped by the transition to the parkland at either end.

Pete and I looked out at this place that was to become our walking turf for the remainder of his life, a place we would return to in all weather and seasons, a topsy-turvy place, a haunted landscape with a sense of humor, a landscape that was wise and world-weary, that had been exploited and now, though marked by its past, luxuriated in benign neglect.

I felt like Robinson Crusoe.

CHAPTER FIFTEEN
The New World

It was like one of those dreams in which you find a hidden wing in your house. You open up a forgotten door or find an unknown stairway . . . and there it is—*all this new space!*

My town had a *wild frontier.*

Or so it seemed to me. Of course, this place, the New Jersey Meadowlands, of which I had discovered a small piece, had always been there. On a topographical map the whole of the Meadowlands appears as a vast pale-blue swatch surrounded by a dense grid of streets, a seventeen-mile-long, four-and-a-half-mile-wide wetlands, stretching out parallel to Manhattan Island. The mirror relationship between the two, which were only three or four miles apart and roughly the same size, was a juxtaposition that writers on the Meadowlands never failed to mention: the great teeming metropolis and the great swampy void standing in bizarre opposition to each other like matter and antimatter.

The Meadowlands is what remains of a great glacial lake that was formed about 12,000 years ago. The icy claw of the Wisconsin Ice Sheet had extended from the Arctic Circle across most of North America, to a latitude that, around here, was even with Staten Island and Perth Amboy, New Jersey. There, warming trends halted its advance. As the half-mile-thick glacier melted, it dropped the rocks and other debris it was carrying, much of it concentrated on the ice sheet's leading edge. This material formed a mountainous dam, behind which the water backed up, becoming Glacial Lake Hackensack.

The end of the last ice age—the Pleistocene Epoch—effectively marks the beginning of human civilization. Only during the warmer Holocene—our present period—did we develop architecture, build cities, invent writing, and make all the other advances that characterize settled societies. In other words, the Meadowlands and human culture share a common beginning. Among the animals that lived around the lake's boggy, fir-tree-lined shores were mastodons, elephant-like creatures related to wooly mammoths, but smaller and stockier. After 2,000 years or so, the still-accumulating waters breached the dam and flowed toward the ocean, making the area to the south of us—central New Jersey—the flat plain that it is today.

Up here, the marshy, former lake bottom became the hunting grounds of the Lenape (Delaware) Indians, a tribe most remembered today for naming Manhattan. They called it Minna-atan, or Island of Hills. Another Lenape band called the Achkinsac (Hackensack) lived on the rise across the creek from where Pete and I were exploring.

Although colonists complained about the Meadowlands from the beginning—it was an obstacle for travelers to Philadelphia, it bred giant mosquitoes, it concealed robbers and even harbor pirates—the land was far from a wasteland. Valuable white cedar trees once grew in it. Trappers took muskrat and beaver pelts. Meadowlands clay (which I began bringing home on my shoes every day) supported a thriving brick industry.

By the time I was growing up in New Jersey, the Meadowlands presented a bleak vista from the highways that crossed it: acres and acres of reeds and mountainous dumps that grew like the Egyptian pyramids. Garbage trucks spiraled up the dumps' earthen ramps and were received at the summit by bulldozers and circling gulls. For a long time, it was the largest garbage dump in the world. During the 1970s, according to Robert Sullivan, in *The Meadowlands*, it absorbed some 11,000 tons of trash every day.

During the 1960s, methane gas from the decomposing garbage sparked an underground fire in the peat that forms the Meadowlands' floor. This fire simmered, smoked, and burned throughout my high school years. Driving through the stench on our way into Manhattan, my friends and I would howl in disgust. I still remember peering out at this blackish wasteland seeping curtains of smoke. It looked like the roof of Hell.

Today that area has shopping malls, an arena, a racetrack, and a football stadium.

Like everyone else, I had heard the stories about mobsters using the Meadowlands to dump all kinds of illegal things, including corrosive chemicals. These chemical pits then became convenient places to dispose of bodies. Most of this is said to have taken place in the industrial areas around Newark, Hoboken, and Jersey City. Our section, at the Meadowlands' northern tip, didn't have such a colorful history. By all accounts, there were no chemical pits or mob-run enterprises in our neighborhood. No underground fires had poisoned the air. But garbage was thrown in there. Lots of garbage.

This didn't happen until well into the twentieth century. As recently as the 1920s, a regional planner described the banks of our broad creek as "one of the finest opportunities for preserving an open space of exceptional beauty in the Metropolitan Area . . ."

Out of this report grew plans for a great marine park where people could swim, boat, fish, picnic, and ice skate. Before the plan got off the ground, a more urgent need was found for the land. A rapidly growing county needed somewhere to dump its garbage. Garbage trucks rolled in for several decades. No one made much of a fuss over this. The towns had been dumping in their own Meadowlands (on a much smaller scale) probably as far back as colonial times. It didn't stop until the 1972 Clean Water Act made it illegal to pollute the river. The landfills were then "capped."

So that was the geology of the land that Pete and I were walking on. On top, a layer of dirt. On the bottom, the ancient clay and peat strata of the old glacial lake. In the middle, about twenty-five feet of trash.

As we were to discover, this place was not only naturally wild, it was wild like the Wild West. Here, for all practical purposes, there were no rules, no authority, and no civilization. There was no need to worry about leashes (after a while I stopped even bringing one), property boundaries, curb rules, and the rest of the upper world's restrictions. There were no police or park rangers.

No law west of the railroad tracks!

As Pete and I began to explore, I was surprised at the diversity of environments. Marshes, I came to learn, were rarely uniformly wet and boggy. They often had sections that were completely submerged and others that were dry and meadowy. They could have dense stands of reeds, swamps, bogs, hummocks—even woodlands.

All of this turned out to be true of these Meadowlands. What looked monotonously unchanging from up on the slope was filled with contrast when you got inside. There were some vistas that reminded me of Dutch landscapes and others that looked like they could have been lifted from Africa. Where the ground was wet or the water table high, the phragmites stood tall, shoulder to shoulder. But if the ground rose only a few inches, they retreated and gave way to ailanthus, birch, cottonwood, and massive willow trees.

At the southern end was a small, dark wood on a peninsula that jutted out into the creek. At the northern end was a bright, sunny wood on a gentle rise. Some of these places were of artificial origin, such as the Rock Pile and the abrupt ridges we sometimes encountered. These berms had been left by the landfill bulldozers, each the terminus of one day's sweep.

The bulldozers had left plateaus, as well. One such area—at the southern end—was covered with low scruffy brush the size and shape of tumbleweeds. We also had our own "Water Hole"—a pool formed by the convergence of streams, where the outflow gathered energy before going out to the creek. The minor turbulence stirred up food, which attracted fish, egrets, and herons, as well as muskrats, woodchucks, foxes, and other creatures. I learned to stay close to Pete when we got close to the area. Otherwise he'd rush ahead and chase whatever was there, leaving me with nothing to see but rustling brush or spreading rings on the water.

I loved the phragmites reeds, which the state Department of Environmental Protection—and the rest of the world, it seemed—branded "invasive" and "opportunistic." It struck me as hypocritical to malign a plant for its ability to adapt to an area where humans had been so egregiously invasive and opportunistic. I found them exotic and beautiful. In a strong wind, their hollow tubes clacked and clicked like wind chimes. In the fall, their plumes turned a plummy shade of purple. I admired their vigor. Within a week after a fire had destroyed several acres of them, the blackened ground was studded with green shoots.

Pete and I moved through their yellow corridors with nothing but blue sky above our heads. Even the floor was a mat of crushed phragmites stems. On first exploring one of these, I would never know if I'd be able to get through to somewhere, or whether I'd hit a dead end and have to turn back. A trail would start out a yard-and-a-half wide, then gradually narrow. After fifty yards or so, the plants would be pushing in on me from both sides.

Sometimes, seized with spring fever, I tried to muscle my way through, stomping down the brittle plants with big clodhopper steps. But this was a project that Pete wanted no part of. A dog forced to accompany a master on such a quest dropped behind with a glum expression that seemed to say, "Want to reconsider this idea?"

Few of the reputed horrors of the Forbidden Forest turned out to be true. We saw no rats or drug dealers, no hypodermic needles or pools of green sludge. In fact, most of the area's hundred-plus acres looked completely natural.

But you couldn't completely avoid the trash. Here and there, erosion had worn down the cap of soil, exposing a collage of broken glass, flattened cans, and automobile tires. Tires, I eventually learned, were particularly buoyant because they trapped a doughnut of air when they were buried. Lengths of cable crept along like errant roots. Muted dolls stuck their heads out of the ground, eyes fixed heavenward, like El Greco saints.

An ancient truck chassis stood upright on its side. Along another trail was an engineless hippie van with a moldy sleeping bag in the back. I developed a fondness for these old wrecks (though I deeply resented any newly dumped things), if for no other reason than that they were familiar and helpful landmarks in the otherwise featureless fields of phragmites.

The most picturesque of the wrecks was a 1960s-vintage Pontiac that tilted nose down in one of the drainage canals. Reeds poked up through its floorboards and open hood. It looked like a giant planter. One day, while we were walking near the bank of a Meadowlands stream, the ground sprung back a bit under my feet. I pushed down with my foot, and the ground responded. I jumped up and down with both feet and the muddy earth cracked open a little, like a mini-earthquake. Down there was something spongy, something like a mattress that refused to compress. Instead of bedrock, a bed?

There were walks where I encountered little or no trash. I didn't really mind seeing one or two things—an occasional refrigerator door or the rusted, half-buried washing machine motor. I'm aware that more fastidious souls would find this stuff intolerable. Those one or two bits of funky scenery would contaminate the rest.

It could even be looked on as an aesthetic question. Did beauty require purity? Did a small bit of ugliness cancel out something predominantly beautiful? In fact, the opposite case was often made in aesthetics—that beauty couldn't exist without ugliness, that each defined the other. Paintings that were too perfect, too exquisite were often judged insipid and cloying. Was it a matter of proportions and thresholds? Would I be turned off if twenty percent of the experience was trash? And what made something *trash*?

One day I spied a translucent snakeskin at the side of the path and picked it up. The snake had been here, had shrugged off its skin, and had simply left it there, like a teenager shedding his clothes on the floor of his room. It was a snake's discard. But it wasn't *trash*. That was because the snake's skin had long ago been incorporated into the natural recycling system. It would decompose or be eaten by another animal.

The refrigerator door had been shed by a human, but nature hadn't found a use for it yet. Given enough eons and enough refrigerator doors, evolution would come up with a solution— some metal-decomposing mold, perhaps—but until then, it would stick out. This piling up of human trash happened because we had moved too quickly for natural systems to evolve in response. Our society made too many things that were trivial and unimportant, like soda bottles, that had life spans more appropriate to a culture's greatest treasures.

Pete couldn't have cared less. Dogs, I recalled, got their evolutionary start picking among the leftovers of Paleolithic dumps. Not that he showed any interest in old washing machine motors or little plastic dinosaurs or 99 percent of the other Meadowlands artifacts that we came upon. He was interested in the more recent castoffs, like the rib bones he sometimes found at a hobo campsite, and which he sometimes smuggled back to the house and gnawed to scrimshaw in a hidden corner.

Nor did the wild animals appear to mind the intrusion of tires, scrap metal, and plastic into their natural world. Woodchucks were fond of the ridges left by landfill bulldozers. They burrowed down into them and then up, creating rooms that were high and dry. In digging, they sprayed out a plume of ceramic and glass shards. Birds used threads from scraps of unraveling carpet for their nests. And the rabbits, as I discovered by following their tracks one snowy day, dug their warren beneath the sturdy roof of a partially buried set of bedsprings.

I began to understand what had happened here. Dumping had stopped in the early 1970s. Several decades went by. Nature works fast under most conditions and conditions in the Meadowlands were much better than average. Sun and water were plentiful. Steady breezes carried in tons of seeds. There was enough soil on top of the landfill to support most growth and enough high ground (where dumping never occurred) to support stands of trees. Most importantly, perhaps, people kept away. What wanted to grow, grew. No one was there to compose or shape nature's progress, to rule on what plants were desirable or undesirable. Animals flourished under the same benign neglect, better protected by the Forbidden Forest than they could be by the most enlightened wildlife management program.

I'm not an expert, but it even seemed to me that global warming, with its wetter summers and carbon dioxide–enhanced atmosphere, contributed to the primeval lushness of this place. Whatever dangers global warming poses for the planet as a whole, it jazzed up vegetative growth in this pocket. Despite the history of abuse, these hundred or so acres seemed as steamy and fecund as a jungle of the Carboniferous Period, 300 million years ago.

A Garden of Eden on top of a landfill.

It never stopped striking me as incredible that all this could be here—this great, open secret of a landscape and that only Pete and I—plus a few joggers, birdwatchers, dirt-bike kids, and various oddball shadow people—seemed to know about it.

Was it romantic to think of it as a wilderness?

Well, by one definition it was. There were places that I was never able to reach. Out in the sea of phragmites were distant hummocks—small, slightly elevated groves of trees. They were remote and unreachable islands. No paths went to these places. Pete and I tried to get through on more than one occasion, but the terrain turned too swampy or the reeds finally defeated us.

I could have brought in a machete, but on reflection I realized that I liked having a part of my world that remained remote. Nowadays we expect every corner of the world to be accessible.

Sometimes I'd look out at these islands and, in a juvenile fantasy, think that if I ever became a fugitive, or for some reason needed a secret refuge, I knew a place where no one would ever find me.

Once or twice, perhaps in trying to reach one of these places, we got lost. That can happen in the phragmites, just as it can in a hedge maze, simply because you can't see over the top, and the paths look so much alike. Nothing takes you back to childhood so quickly as being lost. Your world expands. You feel like a balloon cut loose.

To be lost in Northern New Jersey! In the most densely populated half of the most densely populated state. A mile from the George Washington Bridge! Man and dog in a strange and private wilderness.

Oh, Paradise.

CHAPTER SIXTEEN

The Wild, Redefined

In the Meadowlands, Pete and I were no longer just walkers. We were explorers. Soon, we were using two entrances: the plank behind the pool and the path in from the back of the Grove in Overpeck South. The small parking lot, with its log-and-boulder fortification, became our Outpost. Joe, anchored there by his bad leg, was its crusty old-timer, a fount of trail lore and natural history.

Which way we went in depended on how much time we had, what part we wanted to explore, and whether I was looking for Joe or not. Another variable was the plank, which sometimes washed downstream after a heavy rain and had to be retrieved or replaced.

Occasionally, we saw Korean women squatting in the under-growth along the road, foraging for wild greens. Shy Guatemalan laborers, dark-skinned, short-legged men in sweatshirts and jeans, sometimes walked the road along the railroad tracks, eyes averted, heads down. I wondered what these people's lives were like, what had brought them here.

One day, a ring-necked pheasant erupted from the reeds, so suddenly and with such hysterical chortling that Pete and I practically jumped a foot in the air. Joe knew all about these birds and their sudden ascents—the behavior that made them such popular game with hunters. But I never got used to them, nor understood why, if their goal was to escape, they made such a racket.

Sometimes I'd see a dark upright shape ahead on the trail. It would be the size of a cat, but not the shape of a cat. It flattened when it flopped to the ground and seemed to slither off, always in the direction of water. Then one day I saw one cruising right down the middle of the Water Hole, his wedge-shaped, oily head leaving a neat, V-shaped wake. A muskrat. He sounded the moment he saw me and didn't surface again.

"They have underwater entrances to their lodges," said Joe. He talked about men he knew who had once earned a living trapping muskrats in the Meadowlands.

One bright February morning an owl flew right by me, only a little above my head. I looked right into its owl face, with its big yellow eyes and small curved beak. It flapped its wings soundlessly. In pursuit was a gang—a *murder*—of crows. I'd never realized what big, tough-looking birds they were. They converged on the slower, smaller bird like fighter planes. They rammed him with their beaks, driving him to the ground in a fluttery heap of reddish gold feathers. Then they settled onto nearby branches and waited for him to try to fly again. After watching the sequence repeat itself several times, I drove the crows away with rocks. They flew off, cawing in protest. After a few minutes the bruised and disheveled owl escaped in the opposite direction.

"Crows hate owls," said Joe, as if this were a simple fact of life. He then questioned me about the owl until he satisfied himself that it was probably a screech owl.

I began reading up on the natural history of the Meadowlands. At the time the colonists arrived, and for some time after, these lands were home to beavers, elk, deer, wolves, mink, otters, fishers, rabbits, flying squirrels, bears, and mountain lions. And that's not even counting the birds and different species of fish.

One by one, almost all had been killed off or driven away.

All those animals, so few people. No trash. Everything in perfect balance. And this was not in some remote prehistoric period. It had only been a few hundred years ago, an insignificant span in geological time.

The news wasn't all grim. You could the see the area grow wilder every year. You could sense the presence of more and more animals. Seeing even one wild animal gave me a sense of well-being that I could carry around with me all day. And that, I guess, was partly why I was eager to get the news back to Joe at the Outpost—because with every sighting, progress was confirmed. It was proof that the wheel was turning in the other direction.

But you had to see the animals to know and feel all this. And that was a problem. "The creatures I seek have several senses and free will; it becomes apparent that they do not wish to be seen," wrote naturalist Annie Dillard. It was the curse of the Expulsion. In paintings of the Garden of Eden, Adam and Eve coexisted peacefully with the animals. The Fall changed all that. It not only exposed Adam and Eve to pain and death but alienated them from the rest of creation.

Some wild animals seemed a little more tolerant of human proximity than others, but not because they trusted us. If I got better looks at the woodchuck and the skunk, it was mostly because they were myopic or confident in their ability to defend or escape. Sometimes a sluggish garter snake had to be prodded with a boot tip before it slithered off the path. The carp threw caution to the wind when they were mating, their passions propelling their bodies completely out of the water.

The rest not only fled but also avoided our eyes like lasers. The turtles flopped off their logs the minute our faces appeared between the reeds. Hawks lifted off their branches when we were still more than fifty yards away. The great blue heron was pumping its wings at the first sound of our approach. The frog jumped with an indignant bark. Even minnows scooted away in our shadows.

In observing this phenomenon, I flashed back to the dioramas at the American Museum of Natural History. I realized then what made them so magical—more magical for me than zoos ever were. Zoos were the reality of animal proximity: the animal caged and us peering in. But the best of the dioramas were like the granting of a wish, a wish for things to be as they were in Garden of Eden paintings, where the animals didn't dive for cover at the first sight of a human being. It wasn't a greedy wish. It wasn't the fantasy of animal comradeship, as in Quaker minister Edward Hicks's painting *Peaceable Kingdom*, where the animals cuddle up next to the man like a litter of puppies around its mother. It wasn't a wish to be loved—just not to be shunned.

Pete, despite being my bridge to the natural world, was really not much help with animal sightings. Oh, he took care of himself, all right. He certainly saw—and smelled—more animals than

I did, but he scared them off with his mock-predator charges. One day, I got lucky. We were coming up on the Water Hole, when Pete stopped to linger over a scent. As I turned the last bend and entered the little clearing, I startled a woodchuck. He was standing to my left in some tall grass chewing on the wheat-like tops. He saw me and scrambled for safety, the layers of fat rippling on his back. At the same instant, a red fox flew out from the right, ready to pounce. It was like a collision of three billiard balls. The fox's eyes met mine for a split second before he wheeled about in a soft, fluid motion and disappeared into the reeds on the right. The woodchuck caromed back to the left and escaped to its burrow with a mad scramble of claws.

Pete arrived a moment too late to see any of this. For once, he was the one who had missed the excitement. He knew it. He raced around the clearing collecting the scents that hung in the air, trying to reconstruct what had happened.

I tried to remember everything I had seen. The fox's face was small, its muzzle flatter than a dog's. I felt guilty about interrupting its attack. Ordinarily, my sympathies would be with the prey animal. But the fox seemed so courageous, attacking an animal that was almost as big as itself, especially given what I knew about woodchuck claws. It was a life-and-death drama. Right here in my junky old Meadowlands. A predator, even just a medium-size predator, made this place every bit as wild as the Canadian woods.

Hours later I was still excited about the idea of a fox hunting in the Meadowlands. Of course, I brought the story to Joe, who nodded sagely at every detail. I understood that it was moments like this probably more than the kill that drew men to hunting. It was about being there. For a few seconds I hadn't been an outsider. I'd been part of the diorama: "The Red Fox and the North American Groundhog." I'd been on the inside!

For the first time in my life, I felt as if I had a place in nature. Perhaps that sounds strange: to have discovered nature in a place like the Meadowlands. Hadn't I been in real wildernesses?

Of course. I had seen the great Sequoias, hiked in the Adirondacks and White Mountains, and once, on a Cub Scout camping trip with my son and his "pack," been quite close to some black bears. But these experiences in these places often reminded me of first-time visits to great cathedrals or other architectural landmarks. There was this touristy aspect to it. You knew you were supposed to be full of wonder and appreciation, and your self-consciousness got in the way. It was how I sometimes felt standing in front of some of the more National Geographic–style Hudson River School paintings by Frederick Church and Albert Bierstadt. They left you with nothing to discover.

The Meadowlands, in contrast, didn't expect to be admired.

It was like some big machine that had been left outside to rust. It sputtered, squeaked, and leaked oil, but it kept on running. And I could peer under its hood and see how things worked. I could see why this flywheel was here and why this crankshaft was there. I could see how the machine had been thrown off kilter but was righting itself.

I found myself rethinking my idea of "wild." The world that Pete and I entered may not have been entirely natural, I reflected. Beneath the ground were all those layers of trash, after all. But "natural" wasn't quite the same thing as wild. Wild, I decided, had to do with control, not aesthetics. And wild was what I wanted.

Central Park was beautiful, but it was about as wild as a golf course. It was a masterpiece of naturalistic landscape architecture. Even some of the animals—the turtles in the turtle pond—were transplanted scenery. And the park was regularly groomed and maintained to make sure that nature didn't try any moves on its own. Nothing was supposed to change.

Not only were these Meadowlands acres wilder than Central Park, they were now wilder than any "nature preserve" I knew of. This place had no maps, guide, or master plan, no park rangers, resident botanists, or "wildlife control officers," and scarcely any human visitors.

I looked around at the processes around me. Water percolated up from the ground of its own accord and trickled out to the creek. The phragmites claimed more ground with spiky subterranean shoots. The cottonwoods released blizzards of cottony seeds. In the skies above, gliding hawks and various raptors scanned the ground for mice and other small creatures. Egrets and heron waded in the shallows. Snapping turtles climbed up the bank to lay their eggs. Tiny tadpoles hatched in puddles from eggs deposited by ducks' feet.

Nature going its own way.

So where did we fit in? An art critic and his scruffy poodle? What was our place in this great cranking machine? The answer to that question was as plain as the dirt under our feet. In fact, it *was* the dirt under our feet.

We belonged to the paths.

Despite the muck and marsh and dense stands of reeds, the Meadowlands had a fair number of these trails. They skirted its raised rim, ran along the riverbanks, ambled through the light-dappled woods, and curved through grassy clearings. Some were confident and reliable in all seasons, others tentative and moody. Some appeared literally overnight—the work of nighttime vandals driving their SUVs through the brittle phragmites—and then gradually disappeared over a month of furious growth.

Except for the dirt road along the railroad tracks and its spur to the Rock Pile, all these trails were impromptu and unmaintained. They existed because feet and paws had repeatedly pushed back the vegetation and compacted the soil. This had been going on for eons. Animals migrated. Predators (like the wolf) followed their trails. Primitive people climbed aboard as well, making use of all the trial-and-error movements of their predecessors.

Paths, when you thought about it, were one of the few animal-human collaborations. It was prehistory's greatest cross-species public works project. Humans took over, as they tend to do, turning paths into trails, trails into roads, roads into highways. The beginnings of that impulse could be seen out on our wooded peninsula where some unseen shadow persons—a Boy Scout troop, perhaps—had carefully lined the path with thin logs in the Adirondack-camp style.

And then there was the mother of all paths, the New Jersey Turnpike, always within earshot as Pete and I roamed through the

Meadowlands. It hummed and buzzed night and day—all eight lanes of it and in some places, twelve. Its concrete and asphalt ribbon brooked no obstacle. It rolled across the landscape, over marshes, through cities, under and around other highways, relentless and efficient.

Pete and I shared the common language of trails: Winding trails were about anticipation: *What's around the next bend?* Long straight trails were about routine and practicality—the shortest distance between two points. Woodland trails aroused the slightest wariness. Trails to water were a promise of pleasure.

When a trail ended, our spirits sagged. Some got too dense or tangled to let us pass. There was no path, because there had been no need. No one else wanted badly enough to go this way. Other paths faltered and disappeared because the landscape offered too little resistance to require one. That happened in the small woods on the high ground. As Pete and I climbed, the trees thinned out, until we got to bright clearings where there was nothing left to define a trail. Instead of happiness, we felt unease. Pete sniffed and I looked, each of us trying to pick up the trail. We missed having the path to guide us.

Sometimes, I think paths must have been the birthplace of writing. Certainly they were the birthplace of reading. The trail was always about signs and landmarks. Animals left their signatures. They marked their passage with scat, urine, footprints, heaps of feathers, bits of fur, shredded skins, blood, bones. Every animal or hominid that passed left its mark on the earth, like an endlessly uncoiling scroll. All this was observed, sniffed—*read*—by others.

Pete and I took to this unfurling surface with the same under-standing. We read the trail's data and felt the pull of its narrative, like lines from a story . . . "and so they set out . . ." ". . . and soon they came to . . ." We joined all the other legs and feet on surfaces warm and odiferous with recent passages. I used vision and reason. Pete used vision, smell, and instinct. We were part of a communal enterprise. All equal on the path, each contributing—compacting the earth, breaking a twig, keeping the path alive.

Chapter Seventeen

North

I shared my Meadowlands adventures with Janet and the kids, but I was careful in talking about it to other people. Some people visibly recoiled if you told them you walked in the Meadowlands. Others, you could tell, quietly adjusted their opinion of you, turning the character dial several notches toward "eccentric."

It was the rare person who was genuinely curious and had the right sensibility to appreciate it.

One of these was North, a fellow member of the newly created Historic Preservation Commission. He lived in a landmark Victorian house and taught English at one of the nearby state colleges. At the end of the meetings, we'd sometimes talk for a while on the sidewalk.

"Really?" he said when I told him about the Meadowlands. He'd lived in town for twenty-five years and had never set foot in the place.

I told him about being isolated in the tall reeds, of the hummocks and the rusted wrecks. And then, wanting to convey something of the unusual society it offered, I told him that, just the other day, I'd met a dwarf.

"A *dwarf*?" said North, looking incredulous.

This was true, but not in the fairy-tale way it sounded. He was a contemporary boy with dwarfism, about thirteen, with bright blue eyes and a sparkling jewel in one ear. He and a friend were riding bikes on a bumpy path near the Water Hole. They were nice kids. They stopped to admire Pete and asked permission before petting him.

I never got to tell North the particulars of this story. He had to get to the library before it closed.

"I'd like to join you sometime," he said before he left. "It sounds like Middle Earth."

"Call me," I said.

I wasn't sure if North would call or not, and I wasn't sure if I wanted him to. What if he wanted to come every day? Was I going to get trapped in another dog-walking marriage? Did he even have a dog?

North didn't have a dog, as it turned out. But as he explained to me on the phone, he was supposed to get more exercise for his high blood pressure. On the appointed day, I drove through the winding narrow streets of North's Victorian neighborhood and pulled up in front of his turreted house. Pete, puzzled by this deviation from the usual routine, watched from the car as I went up to the porch and rang the bell.

North poked his head out, as excited as a kid on Halloween. He was wearing a tweedy Sherlock Holmes–style hat and a mottled green coat with a greasy patina.

"How do you like my English walking jacket?" he asked. "I just waxed it."

North, I reminded myself, was a genuine antiquarian. Whereas I valued the town's past, North lived in it, or at least his domestic re-creation of it. He had researched his 1887 house and had decorated it with period antiques. Now he was ready for a gentleman's *walk.* It was like calling on Ralph Waldo Emerson. I mumbled something about the funkiness of the Meadowlands and how the proper outfit might be closer to what he wore to do yard work.

"Nonsense," he said. "And here is the pièce de résistance!" He held up a knobby walking stick. "A genuine blackthorn."

He was having too much fun, I could see. And who was I, a junior Davy Crockett, to interfere with his fantasies?

He went on to tell me about the cane, which had been his step-father's. The old man had belonged to a Continental hiking society. The stick was encrusted with the medallions he had earned in treks across Europe.

He made me admire the medallions. I couldn't help thinking how this cane, that had once traversed the Alps and maybe even the Khyber Pass, was about to make its first trek over ground springy with layers of compressed mattresses.

We climbed into the Roadmaster station wagon. Lately, I'd been keeping the second row of seats flattened. This gave Pete an area comparable to the bridge of the *Starship Enterprise.* It also allowed him to come up and stick his head between the front seats. He gave North a thorough sniffing.

I watched out of the corner of my eye. I was curious whether North was a dog person. Dog people usually give dogs' heads a good rubbing, scratch them vigorously behind the ears, and talk to them. North extended one finger and gingerly tapped Pete on the nose. "Hello there," he said cheerily.

Nope, I thought. Not a dog person.

But North was definitely a Meadowlands person. He didn't care for the part where you walked the plank across the canal, but once over that obstacle, he thoroughly enjoyed himself.

I held Pete by the collar as we tiptoed up to the Water Hole so that he might see some wildlife. We were rewarded with a momentary view of a wading egret and several turtles balanced on a log. I walked North through heath-like scrub brush, out on the peninsula, and through the desolate expanses of reeds. He loved it all.

"I'd like to come again at the end of the week," he said.

North brought great enthusiasm to the walk, though—like Bill Pemberton—not a lot of physical vigor. He was a little thick around the middle and, in those early days, bothered by hip and back problems. He sometimes walked slightly bent over. On cold mornings, a drop of moisture would hang—but never fall—from the end of his nose.

But he was never dull company. He was a brilliant conversationalist, learned and funny, was a good storyteller, loved politics, had an interesting biography, was highly observant, and knew different town gossip than I did. With his patrician looks, his fancy walking gear, and his refined tastes in art and antiques, I thought the junky side of the Meadowlands would put him off. But that wasn't the case. Quite the opposite. Whereas I thought the trick was to edit out the trash, to appreciate the Meadowlands *despite* it, North gave it equal billing. He was like a kid in a junkyard.

It really wasn't a contradiction. He was, I learned, a natural scavenger. He had an eye for the dust-covered treasure. He wasn't rich and had had to hunt for the antiques in his house. A few had even been picked off the street on the twice-a-month big trash nights, when the town picked up furniture or otherwise awkward items.

It was a rare walk where he didn't pocket some treasure: a handful of brass screws, a small blue vial, a carpenter's folding rule. He'd pick up some broken pieces of ceramic that meant nothing to me, turn them over in his hands, and identify them as "electrical resistors." He found things interesting, not necessarily because they were valuable but because they contributed to the historical narrative. He'd find a bottle cap and pronounce it a great find because it was from an old beer like Schlitz. He'd see a small portion of a creamy white bottle, and before getting it half unearthed he'd have already identified it as an Old Spice cologne bottle.

Occasionally, I was irked. I had my own idea of how a dog walk should proceed. Pete and I had developed a rhythm. I'd be marching along, my blood beginning to flow, when I'd realize that North was twenty yards back poking at the ground with that walking stick of his.

He played archeologist. It was like trailing after Heinrich Schliemann in his excavations of Troy.

"Maybe you ought to bring a shovel," I said once.

"I'm tempted," he said. "This upper layer is mostly stuff from the seventies."

I pictured a layer of bell-bottom pants, leisure suits, and disco records.

With North along, the Meadowlands became a paradoxical place, more like Alice's Wonderland than the Forbidden Forest.

The shadow people, finding a bigger canvas to work with, were bolder here than back in our little woods. They didn't just build dams or drink beer. They came to live, cooking dinner on rusted grills and making tents out of rope and sheet plastic. Or they tried to burn down the place.

Some shadow people presented puzzles, such as the one we nicknamed "Tulip Man." This unseen person arranged rocks and old bricks into a small square enclosure around a mound. All winter, we theorized as to its purpose. A burial place for a pet? What could it be? In the spring, succulent shoots appeared. Then stems and plump buds. Tulips blossomed—red, yellow, and pink. We admired them for a day or two until, this being the Meadowlands, they were cut and spirited away.

The Meadowlands teased us with sight gags, such as the shoes embedded in the ground sole-up, making it appear as if someone had gone into the earth head first. Icarus? An angel cast out of heaven?

The Meadowlands fooled us with unnatural things that looked natural—the root that turned out to be a piece of wire, the top of an interesting veined rock that turned out to be a piece of marbleized linoleum. And, just when we thought we were savvy about these illusions, it would reverse them. What was obviously a length of copper cable turned out to be a birch tree root, and what our cynical eyes told us was a bleached and partially deflated soccer ball turned out to be a giant globular fungus.

Once, North insisted we scramble down the river embankment so that he could see the exposed layers. Which we did, and, well, this, finally, was too much trash for either of us—not just a few things wearing through the soil on top but a good ten or fifteen feet of *strata,* layer upon layer of squished-down trash within which you could still make out individual things: plastic bottles . . . tires . . . a washing machine basket . . . an old sewing machine . . . chunks of Styrofoam containers . . . a boiler tank . . . a dog's dish . . . tangled sheets of plastic . . . a rusted tricycle . . . It really was like archeology. Pete went off to wade in the creek, and North and I stood there for a few minutes and stared.

I realized why there were no rats in the Meadowlands. There was not a sign of organic matter. Anything a rat could have eaten had long ago disappeared, been reabsorbed into nature. The rest, well, owing to our society's inventive use of plastics and metals— was still eons away from decomposing.

We said nothing. North made a token inspection of the sewing machine and declared that it was of no interest because it wasn't treadle-powered.

Pete got his feet momentarily entangled in a dilapidated box spring.

North appreciated both the strangeness of the Meadowlands and its beauty. I was always seeing paintings in the scenery, and North generally knew the reference. Near the southern end of our stomping grounds, for example, there was a stand of crack willow trees that had the primitive force of Frederick Church's *Heart of the Andes*. That 1859 painting, which delivered such a jolt of the *sublime* that people reportedly swooned and fainted when they saw it, had jungle, a waterfall, and an ice-clad, gleaming volcano in the distance.

No mountains or waterfalls loomed in the composition that presented itself to us, but the willows' long tendrils looked like the vine-and-moss-entangled foliage of Church's jungle, an ailanthus tree poked up just like Church's palm tree, and the upper branches of a sycamore gleamed exotically white.

·

After the tail end of a tropical storm came through and drenched the Meadowlands, I understood how the Hudson River School painters could see a new Garden of Eden in the American wilderness. I look back at a journal I kept at that time and I find that same kind of excitement—of a world reborn.

What lushness. That tail end of a hurricane left the place like a rain forest. Puddles everywhere. The reeds' heavy plumes brush our bodies. Bright green mosses line the path. Toadstools sprout around the base of a dead tree. . . . Streams cut across the trail. Pete sloshes through every puddle. Tiny minnows dart and flicker in the shallow water. How'd they get in there? There was no water in this spot a week ago. It's like seeing the origins of life. Just translucent slivers with fins and an alimentary canal. Some align themselves with the puddle's barely perceptible current. Others cluster in a still corner. Suddenly there's a chase, and a minnow turns on its side, flashing silver.

Already their lives have drama.

Late in the day or early evening, twilight filled the Meadow-lands' shallow bowl like liquid gold. The scenery mimicked canvases by the Luminists, a branch of the Hudson River School, who favored the broad horizontals of salt marshes and low-lying meadows. At the New York Historical Society, I was amazed to see a painting by George Inness of a salt-hay farm in the Hackensack Meadowlands. It was a sweet, soft-focus painting. There are no salt-hay farms in the Meadowlands today, and certainly no barns with thatched roofs, but it had the same light and the same colors that we saw at twilight.

North had his own stock of references for looking at the landscape. Once, picking up a rotted piece of plywood and finding a mass of pale, sickly stems beneath, he launched into Theodore Roethke's *"Root Cellar,"* a poem about discarded plants that won't quit growing. It ends with two haunting lines:

> *Nothing would give up life:*
> *Even the dirt kept breathing a small breath*

A throbbing freight train on a subzero day elicited a recitation of Walt Whitman's "To a Locomotive in Winter." He did the whole poem even though I couldn't hear a word of it above the racket of the train. It was quite a scene: Pete running along next to the train, the engineer waving out the window like a character in a picture book, and North, eyes aglow, one hand raised pedantically, moving his lips like a silent-movie character.

North was like some long-lost brother. How else to explain the odd parallels in our lives? We had both been only children. We were both half Jewish. Our parents divorced when we were infants. His mother was a sociologist, mine a psychologist. As kids in the fifties, we had both been fans of Zacherley, the satirical ghoul-host of TV's *Chiller Theatre*. We were spiritually nourished in liberal religious traditions—he went to a Quaker school in Brooklyn, I was brought up Unitarian. We came of age amid the folk music renaissance of the early sixties, went to hootenannies, and held hands with girls who had long straight hair parted in the middle.

In adult life, we were both married with two children—an older daughter and a younger son, had both moved to town from New York City, were both do-it-yourselfers with older houses who loved hardware stores and Home Depot. He taught English, I was a journalist. He collected paintings and sculpture, I wrote about paintings and sculpture. We were both interested in town history.

The biggest difference between us was that he was a compulsive worrier. He was always fussing over his mental ledger of worries. The entries were mostly late-middle-age discontents and preoccupations—real, imagined, or anticipated:

"Liability insurance"
"Disability insurance"
"Hip replacement"
"Stock market"
"401k"

"Portfolio"
"Retirement"
"Cancer"
"Prostate"
"Anti-inflammatories"
"Idiotic politicians"
"Nursing home"
"Students with piercings"
"Wills"
"Consumer Reports . . ."

He updated his ledger regularly, moving things from the worry to the rest-easy column, putting new things in the potential-worry column, and sliding potential worries into the real-worry column.

Joe and North made quite a contrast: Joe was like the Canadian woodchopper who visited Thoreau at Walden ("A more simple and natural man it would be hard to find") and North was Thoreau's man of quiet desperation. He was always upping his homeowner's insurance for fear that someone would trip on his sidewalk and sue him. He always bought the extra rental-car insurance even though he knew it was a rip-off. He was aghast at Joe's cavalier attitude toward issues of liability, particularly in the case of a vicious wolf-dog hybrid he once owned.

"He bit about fifteen people," Joe told us.

North's mouth dropped open.

"I would tell them not to pet the dog, but they'd go ahead and pet the dog anyway, and he would bite them." He chuckled. "He gave everyone two bites."

"I'm amazed he wasn't sued," North said, after we were in the car.

"I don't think Joe's friends are the litigious types," I said.

That didn't fit North's zeitgeist. He was a fatalist. Or a stoic. In his view of life, you were always tiptoeing across a minefield. Only vigilance and luck prevented you from getting blown up. Correction: only vigilance and luck could buy you time before you were blown up.

CHAPTER EIGHTEEN

Mafia Graveyard

With North aboard, a new feature was added to the dog walk. After the Meadowlands, we'd drive to the Korean market to have coffee and a roll. I'd buy an extra roll for Pete, and the three of us would sit contentedly in the car and watch the people go in and out. Between us, North and I knew half the people in town. They were all dressed for work, buying their newspapers and their jumbo coffees with sip-tops. They were modern suburbanites, and we, a raffish crew of three, were back from the frontier, out of the swamps, denizens of the Meadowlands.

North was the perfect dog-walking pal, not least of all because he had no dog. I didn't have to worry whether his would get along with mine or whether I'd get trapped in some tedious dog-walking marriage. Depending on his teaching schedule, he accompanied us two or three times a week, so we never got sick of each other.

Plus, he seemed to understand what dog walking was about, that we weren't just out there for exercise, or to give Pete exercise, or even for junk collecting, but that it was about slowing down time, about prying open a space where things could . . . just happen. He needed me to do that for him, just like I needed Pete to do it for me.

North also, I discovered, harbored a curious expectation about our dog walks.

"So when you do you think we'll find our first body?" he asked me one day.

"Well," I said, "this *is* the Meadowlands."

Everyone knew the stories about mobsters dumping bodies in the Meadowlands—even doing the killings there. Personally, I didn't think it was happening anymore. There were too many new regulations, new agencies, and outlandish building projects going on. It was a new era. If the Mafia was involved in the Meadowlands, it was probably as silent partner in some plan to build a dog track or a minor league baseball stadium.

But North was a big fan of *The Sopranos*, in which Mafioso from Northern New Jersey carried out their mayhem in familiar local settings. Segments from one show were shot at our local horse stables, as a matter of fact.

In truth, the sort of remains we were likely to find in the Meadowlands were those of someone's bathroom renovation. But North was right about the link between dog walkers and dead bodies. I did an Internet search and was amazed at how often it happened. Week after week, all over the world, mild-mannered dog walkers crossed paths with those who met untimely and often violent ends. My favorite was the one about the New Zealand dog walker who picked up a boot on the beach and found a human foot inside. Or the Englishman strolling with his cocker spaniel who came upon a decapitated head, a victim of a samurai sword attack.

Of course, joggers also do some of this work, but dog walkers do the heavy lifting, and for obvious reasons. Both dog walkers and murderers frequent the same marginal and deserted fringe places—the murderer because he has a body to dispose of, the dog walker because he doesn't want to have to pick up after his dog. Dog walkers are also often out very late at night or very early in the morning, giving them first crack at nocturnally disposed of bodies. Lastly, the dog's nose is very good at sniffing out corpses that have been carelessly concealed.

Now, if anyone was well suited to find a body, it was North. Not only was he highly observant and a first-rate scavenger, but he gave the impression of having a certain . . . *aptitude* for this sort of thing. For one thing, he lived in a house where a murder had taken place. A previous occupant—an eccentric taxidermist and photographer—was strangled in the backyard by a sailor he had picked up in a Greenwich Village bar. North liked to tell the story of how the real estate agent had tried to put a positive spin on this grisly history: "Well, it's only fair to tell you," he recalled her saying, "that we had a little murder out by the potting shed. But it was very clean—a strangulation—no bloodstains to speak of."

Of course, buying such a house is hardly a determinant of character. But there were other things. Murder and grotesquerie were like minor leitmotifs in his life. He had several friends who wrote murder mysteries, one who wrote books about serial killers and real-life murder cases, and a cousin who'd written a psychological profile of a psychotic whose victims included a nurse from our town. Another friend had written a doctoral dissertation on nineteenth-century "monstrous births"—the Victorian term for conjoined twins, hermaphrodites, microcephalics, and other oddities.

North and I never actually searched for bodies in the Meadowlands. We simply stayed alert to the possibility. Twice, spotting what looked like a body in the reeds, we tiptoed forward with fluttering hearts. Both times the victim turned out to be a Guatemalan laborer sleeping it off.

Then, one day when North wasn't along, I thought I struck the jackpot.

Pete and I had wandered into a small stand of trees that stood in the shadow of the Rock Pile. Most of the Meadowlands is as bright as a beach. This was one place that was shadowy and concealing.

I stepped over a few tires. Pete drifted over to the rocky wall to leave a signature.

Then I saw them. Four mounds of dirt.

What was this?

The mounds were rectangular, roughly six feet long and maybe half that in width. They were about a foot high. An old rusted shovel lay a few feet away. *Could it be?*

Mafia graveyard!

I don't know what I would have thought if I hadn't been primed by North and *The Sopranos*. Anywhere else, such an idea might seem outlandish.

Of course, I was skeptical. These graves, if that was what they were, seemed rather conspicuous to be the work of professional killers. At the same time, the part of me that wanted this to be a bizarre, spectacular find countered with the argument that criminals were often stupid and careless. Maybe they were interrupted. Maybe they were in a hurry to get back to Brooklyn or Jersey City. Anyway, who said this was the work of organized criminals? Maybe these graves were the work of an amateur. Or a serial killer.

In fact, didn't the placement of these burial mounds suggest something ritualistic? I whistled to Pete, who was still busy with dog-communication chores by the wall of the cliff. He came over, sniffed, and showed no interest whatsoever. He declined to even pee on it.

"That's it?" I said. "Aren't you curious?"

He woofed at me in annoyance, and then wandered off to attend to matters he understood.

After a little dithering, wondering if I would be later blamed for disturbing a crime scene, I went for the shovel and began to dig at the foot of one mound. The shovel immediately struck something hard.

Beneath the dirt I could see what looked like bark. I quickly shoveled off more dirt until I could see that the entire mound was made up of logs and stout branches.

It looked a little like a certain kind of art, those pod or cocoon-like structures that were popular in the "post-minimalist" period thirty years ago and were supposed to be about . . . Oh, who could remember or care?

Then I noticed the bicycle tracks. *Of course . . . What an idiot I was.* Mafia graveyard, indeed. These were jumping ramps made by kids with mountain bikes. *Shadow kids.*

Six months later, at the end of summer, a woman's body was found a mere two hundred yards or so from where we regularly walked every day. The story was on the front page of my newspaper. The woman had been stabbed to death. North was away on vacation. It was just as well. He would have been tormented by such a near miss. Technically, the body had been dumped in the Meadowlands—but not the wild, disreputable part of the Meadowlands. This murderer had chosen the North Park, where the running tracks and tennis courts were.

The body had been pushed out of the car at the entrance to the parking lot. Wouldn't you know it? Here in the suburbs even the murderers were loath to get out of their cars.

The case lived up to its tabloid promise: a man leading a double life, married to one woman, engaged to another. The victim, the "fiancée," had found out the truth and confronted him. There was an argument, a struggle, and the murderer stabbed her thirteen times.

A woman from town found the body at 4:30 in the morning. What, the police wanted to know, was she doing out there at that hour?

Walking her dog.

North and I, it seemed, were never destined to find real bodies. But we did find quite a few doll bodies.

They were made of a tough rubbery plastic, so they had never decomposed. And they were buoyant, like the tires, so they tended to rise in the landfill and pop out. Some came up with spookily upraised arms, like zombies rising from the grave. Others had their heads down, ostrich-style, as if they were trying to get back in. Some had been half in, half out for so long that they were two-toned: blackened where buried, bleached where exposed.

Most were disfigured in some way. The skulls of the brittle ones were cracked or shattered. The faces of the pliable ones were mashed and distorted. Mechanical eyes rolled every which way. Dirt plugged empty arm and leg sockets.

Oh, those poor baby dolls. You couldn't help feeling a pang. Once, they had been adored little darlings, pushed around in toy carriages, fed from baby bottles held to their rosebud lips, burped with gentle pats on the back, dressed, undressed, and tucked in. There was a doll that talked when you pulled a cord at the back of her neck—"Chatty Cathy"—and a doll that wet her diaper—"Betsy Wetsy."

Perhaps they had first been passed down between sisters, given refuge in attic trunks, or given to the Salvation Army or Goodwill. But sooner or later, most were discarded and came to the Meadowlands. There, cracked, broken, and smashed, they found an afterlife as monsters.

Normally, I didn't pick things up. North was the scavenger in our party. But one day, spotting a decapitatcd doll's head, I picked it up and showed it to him. After he had admired it, I thoughtlessly tossed it back on the ground. I say *thoughtlessly* because Pete automatically retrieved it. He then did his usual routine, prancing around with it and refusing to give it up. He carried it for the rest of the walk, all the way back to the Outpost and the car. I pried it out of his mouth before packing him into the car, and then impulsively stuck the baby head over the hood ornament.

We drove to the Korean market with our trophy.

We sat drinking our coffees and eating our rolls, watching people's reactions.

"What are you going to do with it?" asked North.

"Maybe I'll sneak it into the Whitney Biennial," I said, thinking of that exhibit at the Whitney Museum that every other spring displayed the latest in cutting-edge art. "I'll leave it in a corner, and see if any of my fellow critics review it."

This gave rise to a running joke. Every time we came across one of these grotesque dolls, we would say, "Another piece for the Biennial!"

The funny thing was that the dolls really did fit the then-current zeitgeist. They were "found-object art," which was *in*. They were "kitsch," which was also *in*. And they were grotesque and vaguely medical, which was very *in*.

North started bringing his digital camera to record how they looked "on-site." He made prints on his computer and gave them to me as souvenirs.

Our most lurid find was a Barbie doll. We spotted her in a shallow inlet of the creek—in mystery-novel parlance, a floater. I can still see her, unclothed, floating on her back. One of her hands was reaching out of the water, the other seemed to be arranging her tangled hair. The crook of her arm had trapped a batch of duckweed—bright green confetti-like flakes. Her bangs were pushed back, exposing a broad, high forehead and the rows of tiny hair holes. Her mechanical eyes stared up at the sky.

North took a whole slew of photographs. The prints looked like the cover of a crime novel.

I never said anything to Janet about any of this. I knew she'd think it was creepy. I stuck North's pictures in a file folder and forgot about them. One night, when North and his wife were over for dinner, the subject came up. Liquor had loosened North's tongue and he was going on about "the baby dolls of the Meadowlands" and "this new art genre" we had discovered.

Our wives had no idea what he was talking about, but one thing led to another, and soon North was urging me to "show them the pictures!"

For some reason—intoxication, I suppose—I did. I retrieved them from the folder.

The women were predictably shocked. They found the Barbie doll one particularly disturbing. Seeing it anew in mixed company, I had to agree. It reminded me of a show I'd reviewed on the kinky 1930s surrealist Hans Bellmer, who made life-size dolls and photographed them in bizarre and provocative poses.

It was no good trying to explain about the art-world joke.

It occurred to me that I had become one of those strange friends of North's. *"This one writes murder mysteries . . . another writes books on serial killers . . . and another collects pictures of grotesque dolls that he finds in the Meadowlands. . . ."*

CHAPTER NINETEEN

Good Bug, Bad Bug

After our walks, I usually went to my office to write. Pete would follow me down and curl up on my office couch. That was the scene on this particular day. I was at the computer. Pete was snoring lightly. I felt something on my side. I lifted my shirt.

Arrgh. There it was. A dog tick. It hadn't attached itself yet. It was still climbing, like a soldier scaling a castle wall.

At least they're slow, I thought to myself. Once detected, they have very little defense against a host with opposable thumbs. I picked it off, marched to the bathroom, and flushed it down the toilet. I peeled off my shirt and turned around in front of the mirror. Then I searched my lower half.

Just the one.

Pete sat up and looked at me. I looked at him. He was trying to get a bead on what I was so agitated about. I was trying to get a bead on how many ticks he might be harboring. His black coat was end-of-the-winter long and scruffy. There could be dozens in there.

Somehow, in the exuberance of spring's arrival, I always forget. I walk around as if I was in the Garden of Eden. Everything is in harmony. The sun feels warm and benign. This phase might last a month. Then we're always expelled.

After disposing of the tick, I tried to go back to work, but I kept thinking about its journey. When had I picked it up? The walk had been a muddy one. Back home, all clothes had gone in the hamper. I had taken a shower. Could a tick have held on through showering and toweling? Had it jumped off and jumped back on again? Had it jumped from Pete to me?

Oh, I hated this. One year, I researched them. It was horrifying. At that level of the animal kingdom atrocities are everyday occurrences. Ticks shove a pointed mouthpart called a hypostome into their hosts. The hypostome has backward-pointing barbs—like a harpoon—and secretes a cement-like substance that glues it in place.

A tick looking for a host crawls up a blade of grass and extends its front legs in a gesture called "questing," which sounds endearing if you don't think about the purpose. It and millions of others wait in this questing attitude, hoping they can climb aboard a body, get a purchase, and suck blood. Most never get off that piece of grass. Some must score three hosts in order to get through their life stages—the tick equivalent of winning the trifecta. It's possible, when reading the long odds they face, to feel sorry for the ticks.

After the initial shock wears off, I think—oh well, I can cope with this. Don't people in the tropics become accustomed to shaking out their shoes for scorpions? What's a little tick?

I change my walking habits. I become careful about where I step and what I touch. Instead of barreling through the reeds and striding through tall grass, I stay in the center of the road or path. I avoid brushing up against leaves or stems. But the paths are always muddy in early spring, so I am constantly faced with a choice between trudging through the mud or skirting the edge and getting into the plants.

No matter how careful I am, however, I can't keep Pete out of the grass and brush, and once he gets in there, he's like a tick magnet.

I once interviewed a landscape artist who sometimes worked in the Meadowlands. Halfway through, I finally had to ask the question that was really bothering me: What did he do about the ticks? His solution was ingenious. He wore sweatshirts and sweatpants and cinched the wrists and ankles with pet tick collars. I couldn't bring myself to do that. Not on a daily basis. I hated the smell of those things, and they came packaged with too many health warnings.

His resourcefulness inspired me, however. I could beat these ticks. One year I ordered a couple of Air Force flight suits from a military surplus store. They zipped right up to the neck and had elastic at the wrists and ankles. But they were made for high-altitude flight and they were stifling to wear at ground level. Plus, they gave me a paramilitary look that I was afraid would scare somebody. I, for one, wouldn't want to see someone coming down the Meadowlands road wearing a camouflage-colored suit with rifle-recoil pads sewn onto the shoulders.

Plus, protecting my body from ticks didn't keep them from coming home with Pete. He was wearing Frontline, the protective green gel, but I kept remembering what Cassandra had told me: *"The ticks jump off the dogs and onto you."* I wasn't sure if this was true or not, but it seemed plausible, and sometimes there was no other explanation for how a tick had gotten into the house.

People who fly-fish or hunt sometimes describe the nightmare of black flies, how their swarming and biting practically drove them crazy. But if biting flies can make people hysterical, ticks can make them paranoid.

What was that tickle, that little itch?

Once I've picked that first tick off my body, I can't help wondering if there's another. Every half hour I'll lift my shirt and peer underneath. Soon I'm doing battle with phantom ticks. You never realize how many small dermatological sensations you experience until you have phantom-tick paranoia.

One night, sitting at the kitchen table, I scratched the back of my neck and felt a little bump. I knew that I had a mole back there, but I couldn't remember which side it was on. My hand drifted over to the other side, and, uh-oh, there was one on that side, too.

Tick paranoia is contagious. It can spread through a family. Maybe Claire finds a tick near Petey's nose. The next thing you know, she's asking you to look at something she feels on her scalp. Then, Alex, lying in bed, will see a spot high up on his wall. He'll lie there staring at it for a while, until he can't stand wondering, and he'll get up on a chair and discover that it was just a spot of dirt. I'll be talking to Janet and her eyes will wander to my shoulder. She'll get that look in her eye. Her hand will go up to my shoulder and she'll flick at something. Soon everybody is walking around with the same look, the expression of the seriously distracted.

I have a cousin, an engineer, who was always trying to keep his golden retrievers from shedding in the car. Once, for a long trip to Vermont, he put panty hose on them to protect his upholstery. He used two pairs for each. They looked like sock monkeys.

I always thought he was a bit obsessive-compulsive for going to such lengths, but as I wrestled with the tick problem, I began to think of him as rather ingenious. One of my own brainstorms was to keep a vacuum in the car. I bought the most powerful cordless hand vacuum available. At the end of the walk, before Pete and I got back in the car, I gave both of us a quick once-over. I felt very clever until, one day, seeing an actual tick on my pants leg, I zeroed in on it with the vacuum and was horrified to see that it held tight to the cloth, even with the vacuum's mouth right over it. I had to keep nudging it with the lip before it finally went in. Soon, I was dealing with the problem on all fronts. To keep the ticks off Pete, I used both the Frontline gel *and* a tick collar. I stocked the car with aerosol tick killer that I sprayed on my own clothes and on the carpeting in the car. I bought a dog-walking wardrobe of light-colored shirts and khaki pants so that I could easily spot any ticks that were hitching a ride with me. I vacuumed the back of the car after every walk. I quarantined Pete in the backyard for at least a half hour after every walk so as to give whatever half-dead or stunned ticks he might be carrying time to drop off. I never went into the house after a walk without first taking off my shoes and inspecting my socks. Then, satisfied that there were no ticks on my outer clothing, I would go upstairs, put every article of clothing in the laundry, and take a shower.

There was a sense of systematic triumph in all of this. *No tick could penetrate these defenses!* On the downside, I was beginning to feel like one of the scientists in *The Andromeda Strain*. Nature was my enemy now. I was thinking more about this little war I was having than the spontaneous joys of a simple dog walk.

At that point, I would throw in the towel and accept temporary banishment. Banishment meant giving up the wild for the meadow, which, for some reason, never had any ticks. Being confined to the meadow was hardly a punishment. We'd once been very happy with it and the creek banks. Tick season didn't last forever. Sometimes they'd even disappear in the middle of the summer if the weather was hot and dry enough.

About three weeks into one of these banishments, North and Pete and I were walking the open meadow. It had been raining for more than a week, but the sun had finally come out. The grass in the meadow was almost shin-high, but the lawn mower men had cut a ribbon next to the reeds to keep them from spreading into the lawn. It made a perfect path for us.

When we got to the blackberry bushes, we reached up and ate blackberries for a while. The river was sparkling. I felt as if we were in the middle ground of a Nicolas Poussin landscape. Poussin painted classical Arcadias. In the foreground, he would put some mythological event, such as Diana turning Actaeon into a stag because he spied on her bathing. In the background, he'd put some grand classical architecture—Greek temples, Hellenistic libraries, and the like. But the middle ground was where he put ordinary life: a person riding a mule, a young couple reclining by a pond, men fishing, swimmers in a pool, a boy taking a cow to market. Those were always my favorite parts and that was how I pictured us that day: two people and a dog walking by a creek in the middle distance. Just when you define something as ordinary, of course, it shows you how extraordinary it is. North nearly stepped on a black snake. The creature slithered off in a series of angry s-curves. That was today's news: that the detested "snake in the grass" could, in fact, be beautiful.

We couldn't pull ourselves away from the plump, warm blackberries. A dragonfly dropped down and hovered. It was the biggest one I've ever seen, with an abdomen as thick as my pinkie. It was a candidate for that gallery in the Natural History Museum where all the creatures are jumbo size—giant wolves, giant bears, even giant beavers.

We searched the bushes like shoppers perusing the cases at a department store. I saw translucent newly hatched praying mantises that could have been miniature origami foldings. Pete was up ahead, his nose to the ground.

"Look," said North.

He was pointing into a bank of lush green between the grass and the phragmites. His finger kept moving.

"Look. Look at all of them," he said.

Now I saw them, little flecks of red, bright against the green. Ladybugs.

"They're everywhere," said North.

I had never seen so many ladybugs. They covered the leaves like candy dots.

I fumbled for my reading glasses. Pete, some twenty yards ahead, turned and cocked his head at us.

The ladybugs seemed sluggish.

"They must have just come out of hibernation," I said, though I had no idea what ladybugs did. With my glasses, I could see the different dot patterns. They were each different.

"Look," said North. "These two are double-decker."

"Mating," I said.

"I don't know . . ." said North.

"What do you mean?"

"I have trouble with the idea of a *male* ladybug."

"Oh, right," I said.

This was a role North sometimes played: the crackpot natural-ist. What he didn't know, he made up. He leaned close to one of the leaves, head cocked like a robin. "I think there's just one ladybug, and it's molting," he said.

"Molting?"

"Look more carefully. The upper one is lighter, it's just a hollow shell."

I gave him a look. I adjusted my reading glasses.

"Well, let's just find out," I said.

"No, no!" said North. "You'll harm it. You'll disturb the molting."

I hesitated, not because I put any stock in North's theory but because, either way, it did seem intrusive.

A smile flickered across the crackpot naturalist's face.

Pete had taken a seat and was waiting for us.

I watched one ladybug make ready for flight. Its spotted shell domed up, split, and flipped forward. Out came twirling black wings. The ladybug rose like a helicopter. When it landed, the wings trailed out the back like an errant undergarment.

"Look at these weird things," North said. He pointed to a blackish-purple insect with gold dots. It was smaller than the ladybugs but looked menacing: a tiny, spiky alligator.

"What are they?" I asked.

"I believe those are wingless flies," said Mr. Crackpot Naturalist. "They're waiting for their wings to grow in."

Pete let out a yip of impatience.

"C'mon," I said to North. "We'd better do our walk before the park police show up."

The next day North was not along. Pete and I followed the same trail. I scanned the leafy plants until I found the ladybugs. There were fewer than yesterday, but they were busier, zipping around like little windup toys. I found another conjoined pair and picked them up without hesitation. Little legs emerged from beneath the top one as it scrambled to keep a purchase on its mate. This was no molt, but a virile ladybugman. He was clearly unhappy about having his lovemaking interrupted.

I tried to return the lovers to their leaf, but the male, his mood disturbed, was having none of it. He popped his wing covers and took off. I followed his brief fluttery flight to a nearby leaf, where he readjusted his flying equipment.

One of the things I like about ladybugs is that you can observe them to your heart's content. They tolerate human proximity right up to the point where you grab them with your fingers. Otherwise, they just ignore you—or simply don't see you as anything important or even alive.

I had that macabre little nursery rhyme stuck in my head: *Ladybug, ladybug, / Fly away home/ Your house is on fire/ And your children will burn."* What was that all about? Children burning? As a kid, I could never picture the ladybug's house. Ants had their ant holes, bees their hives, wasps their nests. But, the ladybug, despite its reputed "house," was never seen to enter one.

And now, all these many years later, I'd discovered—if not the ladybug's house—at least Ladybug Land.

On the way home, I stopped at the library and picked up some insect books. I learned that ladybugs belonged to the order of the Insecta class called Coleoptera, popularly known as beetles. The numbers were staggering. There are some 350,000 species of beetles. One out of every four animal species on Earth is a beetle. Ladybugs alone have 5,000 species. I would have thought maybe three.

I scanned the names: two-spotted lady beetle, convergent lady beetle, seven-spotted lady beetle, thirteen-spotted lady beetle, twice-stabbed lady beetle . . . The "lady" in the name, I learned, dated to the Middle Ages, when pest-afflicted farmers prayed to "Our Lady, The Virgin," and the helpful spotted bugs arrived.

Helpful, because ladybugs feed on plant lice, such as aphids, that sucked the juice out of crops.

So, all that charming busyness, the racing up one side of a stem and down the other, which looked exploratory and innocently industrious to us, was actually the movements of voracious predators. To aphids, a ladybug looked like Attila the Hun.

The origin of the house-on-fire rhyme, I learned, went back to the Old World practice of burning hop fields after harvest: Adult ladybugs would fly away, but their larvae and pupae—the children—couldn't escape.

From illustrations of the two stages in ladybug development, I discovered that the larval stage is the sinister alligator-like bug that North and I had noticed. They were sometimes called "aphid-wolves," because of their voraciousness. They fattened themselves up on aphids for several weeks, molting a couple of times along the way. When they reached their maximum size, they hung upside down, molted into the oblong-shaped pupa, and dangled like socks on the line. They spent a week rearranging their parts before emerging as adult ladybugs.

Once, while shopping for plants at the nursery, Claire and I spotted a cardboard container of ladybugs on the checkout counter. We didn't really need any, but we bought them anyway, as temporary pets. At twilight, as instructed, we released them in our garden. The next morning, we couldn't find a single one.

North went away on a two-week vacation to Cape Cod. Left to my own devices, I equipped myself with a magnifying glass and a mayonnaise jar. There were fewer mature ladybugs every day, and none of the alligator-like larvae. But I spotted some pupae. Two looked vacated, like deflated balloons held to a leaf stem with a little piece of tape. Two others looked like experiments gone awry, as if the occupant had gotten stuck coming out and hardened that way. They looked as dry as old corn kernels.

Nevertheless, I gathered some up and took them home. Under the magnifying glass, I could see the pupa's ridged construction, like the shell of a pill bug. One had a ladybug carapace poking out of the open end, but it looked stillborn.

When I looked down into my jar the next morning, however, a perfectly fine ladybug was crawling around. I thought that I must have inadvertently captured it when I gathered up the other specimens. I couldn't believe that life emerged from one of those dried-out kernels.

But it was unmistakably newborn, very, very light orange, almost yellow. Even its undercarriage, which was black in the mature ladybug, was light orange. It was like a car right off the assembly line. I put a few drops of water in the bottom of the jar. The ladybug crawled through it and got one leg wet. It was so delicate that its leg stretched out limp and useless, bleeding a little bit of new orange color into the water. I worried that it might be crippled, but it pulled out the waterlogged leg, regained function, and began exploring.

The next day, my jar held three hatched ladybugs, fresh as could be. Another day, I saw one that must have just emerged from the pupa. It was glistening wet, a shade of yellow without any spots and transparent wings hanging out to dry.

Eventually, I took them all back to set them loose. Some were slow to emerge. They ran repeatedly around the rim of the jar, stumped by the circular path. When one finally took flight, I felt a swelling of pride, as if I'd launched an offspring. One by one they crawled or flew out. I followed their trajectories to see what they'd do in the natural world and whether they would immediately start acting like regular ladybugs.

Once again I got lost in this miniature world of marauding ladybugs and strange transformations. Minutes went by. Suddenly, I looked up, blinking in the light, and saw Pete watching me curiously.

It was a funny role reversal, like those moments when he was engrossed in some scent and I'd have to double back for him. Except now it was my turn to be the object of consternation: *What the hell is so interesting down there?*

CHAPTER TWENTY

Fishing

The sun is hard on a black dog. His fur absorbs the heat. So on those hot days when Pete and I were out in the meadow, we gravitated toward the banks of the Overpeck. He would wade out a ways, drinking while he walked, then lower himself down to cool off. He'd lie there, his tail spinning like a propeller, until he was sufficiently refreshed. Then he'd start barking at me. This was his way of suggesting that I throw him a stick. "Fetch," a game that he found boring on land, became endlessly amusing when played in the water. If a stick was handy, I'd throw it a few times, but I was wary about stirring up his retriever genes. He could become obsessed. On vacations to a family cottage at Lake Champlain, he'd make the kids throw sticks for him until their arms hurt. Even after everyone had abandoned the lakefront, Pete stayed down there, still barking in hopes that someone, *anyone,* would come along and throw him a stick.

To avoid becoming his stick-throwing machine, I'd retreat to a small L-shaped dock farther along the shoreline. In the beginning he'd follow me out there with his dripping stick, but because the dock's railings prevented him from jumping straight into the water, the game didn't work as well from there.

I liked this little dock. The entrance was nearly concealed by blackberry bushes, so it had a slightly secret air. And it had a terrific view. All the less-than-beautiful stuff was out of sight. No trash or tires, no office buildings or phone towers, no green highway signs or noisy tractor-trailers. Just the creek, and as fine a one as you'd ever want to see. The first time I brought North out here, he was awestruck. The water was high following a big rainstorm and flowing fast and clear, past yellow banks on the far shore. It was a scene that might have been out of the nineteenth century, or even the eighteenth. I was reminded of how these very same Meadowlands were used by the movie industry when Fort Lee was a fledgling Hollywood. People say they filmed westerns here, and my guess was that somewhere back in the silent-film archives you could find shots of men on horseback gazing out from this very spot and pretending to be on the banks of the Rio Grande or the Colorado River.

North shook his head in wonderment. "'You feel mighty free and easy and comfortable on a raft,'" he said.

"What's that from?" I asked him. Ever since he found out that I might be writing something about our walks, North had become a wellspring of literary quotes. This one sounded more familiar than most.

"*Huckleberry Finn*," he said. "After Huck and Jim escape from the feuds and the swamp."

Later, at home, I got out my *Huckleberry Finn* and found the quote: *"We said there warn't no home like a raft, after all. Other places do seem so cramped up and smothery, but a raft don't. You feel mighty free and easy and comfortable on a raft."* Then, I lost myself in passages of Huck and Jim drifting downstream in the foggy night, passing long, dark islands, hearing voices across the water, and coming upon floating houses and wrecked steamboats.

I got to wondering what made a creek or a river so beautiful. I analyzed ours like a painting. I eyeballed its width. It was maybe a thousand feet across at that spot—about two-tenths of a mile. That seemed ideal to me—wide enough that a sailboat could tack across it, and yet not so wide that I couldn't imagine swimming it.

The opposite shore was just different enough, and just far away enough, to reinforce that universal human fantasy that a better life was waiting on the far bank.

On the brightest days it sparkled with such intensity that spandrels of light jumped above the surface.

Plus, it was all moving, from top to bottom. Who could imagine what all that water weighed, or how much went by every minute? It made little sound, and yet what passed every minute was easily the weight of a hundred locomotives. Maybe a thousand.

What was down there?

I used to fish quite a bit, so I took an interest. A turtle paddled into view. It swam with all four legs, gamely maneuvering its clumsy shell. In this upright posture, it looked a little clownish, like a man wearing a sandwich board. It swam till it reached a stick, rested one claw on it, and craned its neck out of the water. It had red slashes on the side of its head—a red-eared slider.

Red-eared sliders were sold as pets in the fifties. Lots of people had them when I was a kid. They were usually the size of a half-dollar and came in a plastic dish that sported a plastic palm tree. According to my field guide, they weren't native to this area, which meant this one was a descendant of a feral ancestor. Out of its plastic dish, it had grown to the size of a dessert plate. It saw me and dove for the bottom. It moved like a speedy underwater paddleboat.

I saw the shadows of fish and followed these up to the fish themselves. They were small—maybe four inches—and hung suspended in the water, trolling their side fins. A bit farther out, carp, some a foot or more in length, grazed lethargically, flapping a tail to angle their heads toward the bottom.

One spring, North and I observed their mad mating season. The males chased the females into the shallow water, all of them thrashing and flapping crazily. We could look out over the broad water and see the splashing in every inlet.

One day I arrived to find two boys fishing. They looked about twelve. They had the worms, the tackle, the poles, but nothing in their bucket. They shrugged when I asked them what they were fishing for.

"Just fishing," they said.

I was thrilled. *Kids who still fished!* It's no small feat for a kid nowadays to escape the electronic grip of TV and video games to do this low-tech thing.

I fished when I was a kid. There's a photo of me at age five, fishing on a city pier on Lake Erie. I'm squinting over my shoulder and you can see my mother's shadow on the ground as she snapped the picture. I didn't catch a single thing that day. I don't even remember a nibble. I just remember dangling my legs over the edge and looking down at the opaque green water and feeling somehow happy just to be fishing.

A few years later, at summer camp, I had better luck. There we fished for bluegills off a small wooden dock like this one. We bought drop lines at the camp store and used balls of soft white bread from the dining room for bait. Lying on my stomach, face above the water, I could watch the fish pecking at the hook. I sometimes caught the same fish repeatedly. The poor creature, hooked and rehooked by my barb, stared up at me with its helpless eye.

While I was talking to them, one of their bobbins dipped below the surface.

"Hey," said the one whose bobbin it was. "I think . . ."

The bobbin stayed down and the line went taut.

"Pull him in," I suggested.

The pole was thin and springy and it doubled over as he reeled. He lifted the pole and cranked. Finally the fish's head broke the surface and a moment later the boy was swinging it over the rail and onto the deck.

"What is it?" he said. "What did I catch?"

Fishing

{181}

The fish had a white belly and whiskers, like a carp, but a broader face.

"It's a catfish," I said.

"It's got a moustache," said the other boy, and this struck them both as hilarious. Pete, hearing all the commotion, had returned, and, as often happens when a fish is flopping around on loose line, things became a little chaotic. The boys were sure they would "get stung" by the whiskers and spines, and Pete had to get his nose in there, but finally, I got hold of it and wiggled out the hook, which was cleanly through the lower lip and easy to remove.

We put some water in the bucket, and put the fish in it, where it swam around in circles, looking none the worse for its ordeal.

"You're not supposed to eat the fish you catch here," I told them. Their expressions showed they had no intention of doing so.

"Before you leave," I said, "it's nice to throw them back in."

For me, dog walking is a lot like fishing, minus the fish, which sounds like a joke but isn't—unless you're convinced that fishing is primarily about catching fish. Even on a good day, a fisherman spends most of his time waiting. In the process, he begins to notice other things. The fly fisherman watches his line belly and drift and is seduced by the clouds and treetops. The man standing at the ocean's rim exhales his confined self and inhales the vastness that drew Melville to sea. Eventually, the fisherman discovers something spiritual or transcendent in fishing. He acquires a Zen-like calm. He begins to talk about nature's "temple." The bible of fishing, Walton's *The Compleat Angler*, is subtitled: "The Contemplative Man's Recreation."

My fishing career went in reverse of the usual pattern, like a film run backwards. I started with the fishing enlightenment experience, became philosophical about fishing, fished a lot, and then fished a little.

Many years ago, stranded by a car breakdown, I walked out onto a pier in Virginia Beach. I had been driving home from a visit to the Outer Banks when my car's alternator failed. My car was an old Triumph and the part had to be ordered, so I found a motel and went out that night to explore. I wandered through an amusement park and then paid a dollar to walk out on a fishing pier.

The shore must have had a very gradual slope because it was a very long pier. Out in the darkness, far from the lights and sounds of the amusement park, I came upon some people. A woman was throwing a pyramidal cage over the rail and pulling up blue crabs. Men with poles were casting shiny metal lures and jigging with big gobs of bait. I watched a skinny old man in a blue mechanics shirt pull a big fluke out of the water, flop it down onto the decking, and proudly say "Now, there's a real doormat."

I looked into everyone's buckets, saw more crabs and fish of different sizes and shapes. Everyone had caught something, which made them happy and sociable. Children scrambled across the deck after errant crabs. The adults swapped tips and recipes. The waves lapped against the pilings. From the beach came the far-off sounds of calliope music, the clackity-clack of the roller coaster and the faint cries of its thrill-seeking riders.

In contrast the scene on the pier seemed ancient and profoundly human. These people were just ordinary weekenders, yes. They weren't Biblical figures, like Simon Peter, Didymus, and the sons of Zebedee on the Sea of Tiberias. But they were pulling fish from the sea as people had always done, with tools that have changed little for millennia.

When I got back to New York, I tried to paint this experience. The scene had seemed magical to me—the moon, the lapping waves, the children playing, the fish dangling from the ends of lines—even the distant amusement park. I was a little worried that in painting a subject like this, I could wind up with something out of *Field and Stream*. So I avoided realism—not that I was ever much of a realist—and tried to keep the symbolists in mind. I thought of Edvard Munch and his allegorical *Dance of Life* and Paul Gauguin with his mysterious Polynesian scenes.

I struggled with one big painting until its surface was as bumpy as an asphalt road. When friends came by to look, I wasn't sure they would get it. So I talked nervously about the metaphorical quality of fishing—this reaching down into the unknown, about fishing as an act of hope—or faith—and fishing as this intimate connection with nature.

They nodded. They looked interested and excited.

Had I succeeded?

I wasn't so sure. Everyone wanted to go fishing.

Oh well, why not, I remember thinking. If you paint people fishing and people want to do it, you've succeeded on some level. We were all stir-crazy, anyway. Some hadn't been off Manhattan

Island for a year. It seemed a jolly thing, a bunch of artists going fishing. Eight or nine of us piled into someone's van and drove out to Sheepshead Bay in Brooklyn. There, we signed up for a party boat that advertised, "Blues! Blues! Blues!"

This turned out to be nothing like the transcendent experience I'd had on the pier in Virginia Beach. This was more like being on a pirate ship. The trip took hours. People got drunk and seasick. We anchored above an underwater canyon that the mates called "The Mudhole." The boat, no longer steadied by forward motion, began to pitch and roll. Lines dropped into the water. My line seemed to drop forever before reaching the bottom. I hauled it up a foot or two and waited. The action began almost immediately. The bluefish, once hooked, made wild desperate runs along the length of the boat, tangling everyone's lines. Pulled out of the water, they were powerful tubes of muscle with teeth that chomped right through jeans.

It was four in the morning when we got back to Manhattan. We each had a few gutted fish wrapped in newspaper. Our clothes were stained with blood, slime, and scales. Around the city, wives woke up and said, "What's that smell?"

But we kept fishing. We discovered Sandy Hook and learned to surf-cast on the beach. We rented boats and drift-fished in the bays and rivers. Janet and I rented a cottage and everyone visited. Now and then, I tapped into that vein of inspiration I'd found on the Virginia pier. A childish happiness would well up in me at the prospect of going fishing. My fingers would tremble as I attached the silvery lure or put the bait on the hook. I loved its puzzles and uncertainties—even the silly lures and gadgets. I'd wonder over the tugs, forces, drags, and currents. Was that the bottom? Was that a nibble? Is my bait gone? Should I yank on the line? What am I pulling to the surface?

You never know what it will be. Years later, eager to introduce my kids to fishing's mysteries, I took them out on Lake Champlain. Claire hooked a monster on her "Snoopy" fishing rod, a thick, writhing eel with multiple gills and an angry mouth. It flopped and slithered in the bottom of the rowboat. She and Alex cowered in the stern and begged me to throw it back. Which I did.

Fishing and dog walking have a lot in common as it turns out. Both are about that feeling of setting forth. Both are about having time to waste and nothing special to do. Both are about having "broad margins" to your life. Both usually involve friendships and camaraderie. Both are about solitude, patience, alertness, and dreaminess. But above all, both are about making *contact* with nature.

All I know is that there are days heading out with Pete when I feel as happy as that barefoot boy out of countless calendar illustrations. He's got the grass under his feet, a bamboo pole on his shoulder, a bucket of worms in one hand, a sandwich in his back pocket, and, of course, a dog leaping next to him.

CHAPTER TWENTY-ONE

Disappearing Act

Back when we still walked in the Mystery Trails, Pete and I were startled by some boys on mountain bikes. They came barreling down the gully-like trail bouncing in their seats and whooping like broncobusters. Pete always had an irrational fear of people on bicycles anyway, and these kids spooked him. They were gone in a matter of seconds, but so was he.

It took me a little while to realize that he wasn't coming right back. I spent a half hour in frantic searching, hollering until I was hoarse. I couldn't be sure which side of the woods he had gone out of—one side was a different town. In desperation, I ran back home to get the car. On arriving, I found Pete calmly sitting on the front steps.

Of course, I should have known. He could be spooked, but he had good common sense.

I developed such faith in that common sense that, having trained him to walk on the sidewalk, I dispensed with the leash entirely on late-night walks around the neighborhood. I trusted him not to stray off the sidewalk, even in pursuit of cats or squirrels. I was even a little vain of our ability to do this.

This worked for seven or eight years. Then, around age ten, he began to dawdle. He started ruminating longer over other dog's scent markings. Only after much deliberation did he lift his leg and dribble a bit of his own urine on the spot. Then he would sniff his own marking to determine whether he had said what he had intended to say or said it emphatically enough. Then he would correct or amend, sniff again, and sometimes have to go back a third time. By then, I would often be a block ahead of him, lost in my own ruminations. And so the gap opened up between us.

Around this time, something similar was happening in my marriage. There are oscillations like this in all marriages, I think, or so we were led to believe by our marriage counselor. She was a large-boned, earnest woman whose office had a wall-size photomural of an autumn woodland path. She sometimes munched on carrots or celery as she listened to our problems. Between that and the woodland background, I sometimes felt like we were being counseled by a giant rabbit.

Her metaphor for the bond between men and women was that of a rubber band. The issue, as she saw it, was how much "stretch" there was in the marriage. Some marriages, when subjected to stress, were brittle, she said, and broke right away. Others bounced back.

The dog walk, of course, absorbed a lot of my brooding on this matter. Had I thought about it, I might have reflected on the significance that Pete, Mr. Family Glue, was now frequently lagging so far behind me that I lost sight of him altogether. I sometimes had to double back, where I would find him, his nose deep into a hedge, or balanced on three legs like an unstable tripod while he anointed the roots of a London plane or Norway maple.

So it happened that one moonless night I came up the steps of our house and paused, as I often did, to give Pete time to catch up. Instead, my wife came to the front door to tell me that Pete was at the police station. The authorities had called, she said, "at least ten minutes ago," and would I please go down to the station and retrieve him? I was astonished. I kept looking back over my shoulder, expecting to see Petey emerge from the darkness and straighten this matter out. Janet, who might have otherwise accused me of negligence or some mental deficiency, took an amused, compassionate view of my befuddlement. In retrospect, that general tolerance has probably been a major contributor to "the stretch" coefficient in our marriage.

As I set off for the police station to get Pete, I was still skeptical. It seemed logistically impossible. I scanned both sides of the street as I drove, just in case there was some mix-up. I checked my watch. It was 11:00. I'd gone out at 10:30. It would have taken a while for Petey to fall far enough behind me for the police to pick him up without me noticing. And, according to my wife, they were already calling the house by 10:50. Once they picked him up, they had to drive him back to the police station, process him there, find our phone number from his license, and then call the house to say that they had him. It didn't seem possible for all these things to have transpired in so short a time.

For one thing, it suggested a police force that operated with commando-like efficiency. I had the opposite impression of our suburban police department. They had their good points. They were polite and forgiving about minor traffic violations if you were from town. But they didn't strike me as an organization capable of swooping down out of nowhere and spiriting away a stubborn poodle from behind his owner's back.

My drive to the police station took three minutes and forty-one seconds, which included stops at two traffic lights. I had become very curious as to how long certain things took. This whole business of Pete being in one place and then suddenly being in another reminded me of "The Transported Man Trick." This was a classic magician's illusion in which a man is seen to be instantaneously "teleported" between two booths on opposite sides of a stage. The illusion, I had learned in a recent movie, relied on trap doors under the booths and a double who would appear in the second booth after his twin dropped through the floor of the first booth.

This line of reasoning led to a two-poodle theory. But before I could fully wrap my mind around that concept, I pulled into the police department parking lot and spotted Pete. He was chained to a post outside. I was glad they hadn't put him in a cell, knowing how he had once felt about the crate. He wagged his tail when he saw me. I got out of the car, patted him, and went inside to face the music.

I thought the police might give me a summons for allowing a dog to run loose. I had decided to tell them that the clip on Pete's leash had malfunctioned, but the desk sergeant only asked me to sign some papers. As I signed, I innocently asked how they had come upon my dog.

"One of your neighbors called to report a stray," he said.

There was a big welcome for Petey when I got home. Marital tensions were forgotten for the moment and all four of us sat at the kitchen table to celebrate his return.

"I still can't understand how all these things could have happened in such a short time," I said. "First the lady had to see Petey—"

"What lady?" Janet asked.

"The police said a neighbor lady called."

"I wonder who it was?"

"Some busybody," I said. "Anyway, that just adds another step. She has to call the police, talk to the dispatcher. The dispatcher then wants all this information—you know how they are . . ."

"That's true," said Janet. "Your neighbor's house could be burning down, but first they need the spelling of your name."

"Right, and they must have asked for a description of the dog," I said. "Finally, after they had done all that, they would dispatch a car. Then they have to locate Petey—a black dog on a dark street—and get him into the car."

"That's the part that surprises me," said Janet. "How did they get him in the car so easily? Wouldn't he try to run away?"

"Oh, you know Petey," said Claire. "He loves everybody. He probably got right in the car."

"He hates cars," said Alex, harking back to a tendency Pete had, and which Alex once shared, to get carsick on family trips. It was the bond of the queasy.

Claire turned to Pete, who was following the conversation closely given that every other word was Petey. She asked him how the police got him in the car.

He looked around at all the questioning faces and woofed noiselessly.

By this time I'd gotten a pencil and paper.

"What are you doing?" Janet asked. "Are you making a report?"

"I'm just trying to figure out this time thing," I said. "It's a mystery to me, it really is."

Janet poured us each a glass of wine and I began to plot out a time line beginning with the moment I left the house at one end and the time I got back at the other end.

"I wasn't gone more than a half hour," I said. "You said the police called ten minutes before I got home. And there has to have been some time at the beginning of the walk before we got separated. That had to be another ten minutes. He probably did his serious business first, before he started dawdling over scents —"

"What do you mean, 'probably did his business?'" said Janet, looking at me with narrowed eyes.

"Well . . ." I said.

"Oh, now I understand," said Janet "You let him trail along behind you and poop on people's lawns while you pretend not to see. That's how you lost him."

"I didn't lose him," I said. "He was abducted."

"And now we know why."

"He doesn't poop on people's lawns," I said.

"How would you know?"

"Well," I said, fidgeting a little. "You know the empty lot next to the big house up on the next block?"

"The one that's for sale?"

"Yes," I said. "It's all wooded and thick with leaves. We always go that way first and Pete disappears in there for a while."

"Okay, okay," said Janet. "Finish your chronology. I want to see how this works out."

"All right," I said. "If you take ten minutes off the beginning of the walk and ten minutes off the end, then everything has to happen in here." I point to the bracketed part of the time line.

"In ten minutes . . ."

"Right, the busybody sighting Pete, her call to the police, the police dispatched, the capture, the drive back, the processing . . ." For every one of these events I put a little line across my time line, until the middle part looked like a drawing of a comb.

"It's impossible," I said. "There had to be two dogs."

Both kids were laughing at me now. In fact, we were all laughing.

It was a happy night. I didn't want it to end. And maybe that was why I somehow managed, with Pete's help, to replicate the whole thing about three weeks later: Pete's mysterious disappearance, the alleged busybody lady, the police, Pete taking the perp ride . . .

I wish I could say that we shaved some minutes off our previous time. But this one lacked the finesse and split-second timing of the first one. I think the police were to blame.

This time, I noticed that Pete was gone, I doubled back, couldn't find him, began to suspect foul play, rushed home thinking to myself: "It couldn't have happened again. It couldn't have happened again." This time Janet wasn't waiting and there had been no call from the police.

I had to call them, but, sure enough, they had Petey, and I brought him back. Everyone was as disbelieving as I was, and hugged and patted Pete again, just as before.

But I think my family suspected me of staging it just to get the attention, because they all had things to do when I sat down at the kitchen table to calculate the odds of it all happening again like that.

CHAPTER TWENTY-TWO

Skunk Summer

Humans may have weak olfactory powers, smell may be our "inarticulate sense," but no one fails to recognize that vile cocktail served up by skunks: one part sulphur, two parts burning rubber, one part bear's armpit. That summer, hardly a night went by when we didn't smell that noxious amalgam. There must have been a skunk population explosion in our town in spring. No one remembered there ever having been such a problem in the neighborhood.

When you smell skunk out in the country, it's usually because one was run over. But in the suburbs, where the skunks' predilection for rooting in people's flower beds and lawns increases the chances of skunk-human or skunk-dog contact, skunks do a lot of defensive spraying.

Internet sources say that skunks will stamp their front feet in warning and even hiss before they spray, but I've never noticed either. I have, however, seen them twist around in a horseshoe shape and lift their tails straight up in the air. Only a fool isn't running by that point. Or certain dogs.

Every dog owner hopes that his dog will divine the skunk threat without having to learn it the hard way. I had high hopes for Pete, a dog of more-than-average intelligence. But he continued to regard skunks as potential playmates.

Despite what I'd read about skunks being crepuscular—active in the dusky hours—our suburban skunks were decidedly nocturnal. This, I imagined, was an adaptation to human society's rush hour, a dangerous environment for a slow-moving crepuscular animal whose primary defense involves standing still and raising its tail. Whatever the explanation, we typically saw skunks well after dark. So Pete and I adapted. If the skunks were going to be nocturnal, we would become crepuscular.

Being crepuscular, however, necessitated a change in environment. Our leashless style of walking was poorly adapted to a neighborhood where people were still out and about. So we migrated to the meadow in our old park, open till sundown.

I grew to like twilight, this hinge between night and day. Dog walking is such a simple thing and yet its few variables—place, weather, and time of day—make for infinite variety. Pete seemed at home in it, too, which made sense, since his ancestors, the wolves, were—and are—crepuscular hunters. Colors were richer, deeper in the softer, less direct light. Time itself seemed to change tempo, slowing in the long leadup to sunset, then quickening in the final rush toward darkness, like rapids before a waterfall. The birds sang their evening songs. Rabbits came out into the grass. Swallows darted. So did bats, which looked like swallows until you noticed the little perturbations in their swoops. Fireflies appeared in the gathering dusk. As kids we called them "lightning bugs." They flew so slowly and at such a low altitude that even little kids caught them easily. Softhearted children treated the bugs like temporary pets. They freed them after capture, or kept them briefly in mayonnaise jars. The more callous children casually pinched off the insects' illuminated abdomens to make rings and necklaces. It was the beetle's anatomical misfortune that this little piece of phosphorescence stayed attractively lit after its life was winked out. It was as cursed by human aesthetic preferences as the ladybug was blessed.

The meadow's wide sky gave me clear views of the moon. Before then I had rarely known where in the sky the moon would be on any given night or what it would look like. Our steep neighborhood streets with their high horizons and dense tree cover provided me with little more than glimpses of this furtive body. Who knew if it was even up? It kept ridiculously irregular hours. It went through more phases than a teenager. Sometimes I'd see it wandering forlorn and ghostly across the daytime sky.

Now, with nothing between me and 360 degrees of horizon, the moon began to seem much less capricious. It rose in the east about an hour later every day and was either waxing or waning in its phases. Pretty soon I knew what to expect on each successive night. Still, the moon could startle. One night, before driving home, Pete and I made a detour to pick up Chinese food. The trip took us along the western ridge of the Meadowlands, the same area, I remembered, that had once been home to the Hackensack Indians. Now it was a tree-lined suburban street. Through gaps in the maples, I could see across the Meadowlands to the Palisades, which hid the city beyond. Rising just over the lip of the cliffs was one of those gigantic moons, like the Harvest Moon, though its season was still months away. It was unambiguously full and blown up like a red giant. I knew its size was an illusion, but what an illusion! It looked three times as big as a regular moon. At the bridge over Route 80, a man aimed his camera at it through the chain-link fence.

By the time I had turned east onto the road that crossed the Meadowlands, the yellow orb was blindfolded, a thin gray cloud pulled across its eyes. It looked like a surrealist's stunt, a photograph by Man Ray: "Moon Having Its Last Cigarette At Sunrise."

One night Joe showed up in the meadow parking lot—the old Outpost—just as we were about to leave. In the summer, Joe traded his serious hunter look (plaid hunter's cap, goose-down jacket, and subzero Sorel boots) for an almost frivolous beachcomber look (shorts, a too-small T-shirt tenting over his gut, and moccasins). It was just getting dark, but I hung around to talk. I hadn't seen Joe for a while—he'd been on a fishing trip in Florida. He let Mike out and the two dogs ran off into the gathering darkness. Joe lit his pipe and began to chronicle his adventures at sea.

After a while, I noticed that Mike had come back without Pete. I peered into the dark meadow. As my eyes adjusted, I made out his dark silhouette. He was on a grassy rise and circling, the way he did with a playmate. My heart sank.

"Pete," I yelled. I started trotting across the meadow. As I got closer, I could see the other animal—and its white stripe. The tail was up. It was scooting backward. Pete was leaping evasively from side to side, having a great old time.

I started running toward him, hoping to get him out of there. Before I was halfway to him, he was running back toward me, shaking his wooly head.

I couldn't tell at first how badly he'd been sprayed or where. He ran wide circles around me, rubbing his face and shoulders on the ground. I called to him. He came with his tail between his legs, confused by the disapproval he heard in my voice. Once at my side, he wiped head and nose on my pants leg.

"Come on, Pete," I said, taking pity on him. I imagined him humiliated and disgraced by the skunk's spraying. "Back to the car."

Hearing no more blame in my voice, he started madly dashing around. What was going on with him? Was this some kind of canine hysteria, or was being sprayed by a skunk now cause for celebration?

Joe was shaking his head when we got back to the parking lot. Mike was already quarantined in the front seat of his camper truck.

"That was a mother skunk," he said. "I've seen her around with her kits."

I shrugged, in no mood for a wildlife discussion.

"Tomato juice," he said.

"Right," I said. "I know."

Joe offered me an old blanket to put in the back of the car.

"Just throw it away when you're finished," he said.

I spread the blanket in the back for Pete and let him jump in. I left the tailgate window up. By the time I got into the driver's seat, the smell had expanded to fill the car.

I started the engine and mashed down on the four power-window buttons. When we got rolling, and Pete was downwind, the situation improved a little. Once home, I put him in the backyard and went into the house to break the news to the family. I found Claire at the computer and Janet reading a book.

"Pete got skunked," I said.

"I can smell it," said Janet. "Are you skunked, too?"

"He wiped some of it on me," I said. I related what had happened in the park.

"You had to go to the next town to get sprayed by a skunk?" Janet asked.

Claire went outside to look at Pete.

"He's running all around like a crazy dog," she said, when she returned.

We went into action. Claire was dispatched to the supermarket for tomato juice. Janet and I pulled the galvanized tub out of the garage and set it up on the deck. I soaked Pete with the hose, and then washed him with shampoo from our shower. It was coconut-scented. I applied the tomato juice like a conditioner.

Pete cooperated the first time. But he shook violently in response to the second tomato-juice rinse. Twice he hid under the picnic table. It was an hour before we hosed him down the last time and toweled him with rags.

Alex came home and heard the whole story.

Janet and I finally had a chance to sit down. Pete slowly regained his spirits. Claire gave him a fresh rawhide to chew.

It was after midnight. A breeze rustled the trees. Overhead, the peepers and crickets—or whatever they were—sang and buzzed to one another. It didn't matter that it was late. No one had to get up in the morning. It was summer.

"We must have looked like a Norman Rockwell illustration," I said to Janet. "The dog sitting in the tub. The family members scrubbing, their noses scrunched up. He would have titled it 'Skunked.'"

"What happens to animals in the wild when they get sprayed?" asked Janet. "How do they get rid of the smell?"

"I'm not even sure it bothers them," I said. I recalled something I'd once read about dogs that rolled in smelly things. Dogs with this habit would throw themselves on a dead raccoon or a fish and roll on their backs till they were covered with the odor. Dog experts didn't really know why they did this. There were a few theories. One was that this was a remnant of a hunting strategy in the wolf. The wolf took advantage of such alien scents to sneak up on its prey. The other theory was that this was a social-aesthetic behavior, a way for dogs—connoisseurs of frightful smells—to try one on. Pete stretched out on his side in the grass. Lily the cat tiptoed up and raised her nose over him, sorting out the odd layers of scent: dog, skunk, coconut, tomato juice. Pete permitted the inspection, sighing loudly at one point.

Maybe he wasn't grateful at all for being cleaned up, I thought. Maybe he felt deprived of something.

"Well, at least he understands about the skunks, now," Janet said. "He's learned his lesson."

"I don't know," I said, remembering a story of Joe's about a dog that kept getting sprayed over and over again. I thought then that it must have been a very stupid dog. Now I wondered.

I tried to put myself in Pete's place, tried to imagine feeling giddy at being newly coated in this alien odor. Did the wolf in him rejoice at being so disguised, a predator who could creep up on others as if invisible? Was it like that or more like a child in a Halloween costume?

Either way, I supposed, there had been the excitement of transformation. For an animal with his nose, scent was tantamount to identity. Briefly he'd been someone or something else. What better adventure?

CHAPTER TWENTY-THREE

Luke

When Janet and I lived in Manhattan, we noticed a phenomenon among our child-rearing friends: Those who had only one child continued to live in the city, while those who went on to have a second child soon moved away. It was easy to see why. They added up the cost of a two- or three-bedroom apartment versus a one- or two-bedroom apartment, factored in the second nursery school tuition and assorted other expenses, present and future, and began to think of another way. Soon they had departed to Brooklyn, Long Island, Westchester, or New Jersey.

Years later, long after my own family migration had confirmed this principle, I recalled it and wondered how it might apply to having a second dog. Would there be some hidden cost or difficulty that I hadn't anticipated? Would it be harder to walk two dogs than one? Did I realize that I was extending my dog-walking term of duty out another ten or fifteen years? Would I still find it so interesting and rewarding long after the children had left home?

Had you asked me then why I was getting another dog, I would have said that I was getting it for Pete. It began with an injury. He came back from a trip to Vermont limping on his back right paw. It didn't bother him in the house or on grass—just on rough ground or gravel. Had something gotten lodged in one of his pads? It seemed that way. When I pressed on the bottom of that foot he put his mouth on my hand and growled a little to warn me off, and yet, several vets had probed and x-rayed the area and found nothing to remove. Each counseled that we wait a little to see if it might take care of itself. But it didn't. After about six months, we were referred to a specialist who recommended amputating the offending toe and pad.

The operation was expensive—$1,500—and left Pete with a three-toed foot on his back right leg, but it restored his normal gait.

In the process, I noticed how much he had aged. His black coat was nearly all gray. His face had hollows, and his trunk had bulked up. Even with his foot repaired, he wasn't the old Pete. I missed the unpredictability, that poodle *joie de vivre,* the animation that he always brought to our outings.

He had recently turned ten. That was seventy in dog years. Seventy!

I had been thirty-nine when we got Pete; Janet, thirty-eight. Alex had been four and Claire seven. Add ten to each of those, and Janet and I were deep into middle age, Claire was seventeen, a young woman, ready to leave home. Alex was a strapping fourteen-year-old who could throw a baseball so hard it hurt my hand to catch it.

But Pete—in the common seven-to-one ratio of dog-to-human years—was older than any one of us. By the eleventh year, I realized, he would be old enough in human years to be my father, and by the fourteenth year, my grandfather.

And yet, he seemed healthy and certainly had some good years left. Like me, he was at the two-thirds mark in his projected life. I didn't feel old. Why should Pete feel old? And wasn't it commonly said that a puppy could restore an aging dog's playfulness? So, I began to float the idea of a new puppy.

Ideas like this need to build momentum, and for many months it was just a fantasy. Claire, the family's number-one animal lover, had her sights set elsewhere. She was on the threshold of independence. She wasn't thinking about puppies and family life. She had an academic year to finish and college applications to fill out. Lots of applications. There were essays to write, test scores to assemble, and financial-aid forms to fill out.

Janet and I couldn't believe how expensive college had become. There seemed no way we could afford it without lots of financial aid. And so, we, too, had lengthy applications to fill out. To me, it still seemed semi-miraculous that we had gotten this far—had managed to buy a house and to raise the children in a nice community, had dealt with all the childhood illnesses, the orthodontia, the summer camps, the ever-more-elaborate birthday parties, had coached teams, gone to school plays, and all the rest of it—only to arrive at childhood's end and find a bill for the biggest item of all.

In this atmosphere, with shaky finances and an adolescent under more pressure than she'd ever been under in her life, was it surprising that a puppy seemed a sweet and desirable thing? Family glue! And rejuvenation for Pete!

In idle moments at the computer, I searched the Internet for poodle breeders. Soon I had found one that seemed affordable, not too far away, and pleasantly quirky. She was in Catskill, New York. The Web site displayed a picture of a big, multiturreted Victorian House. The next displayed a carefree glamorous couple riding in a red convertible with a white poodle between them. Now, there was the life!

The site had the usual poodle-promotional language, extolling the breed for its near-human intelligence and finely tuned sensibilities. Its tone suggested that, in acquiring a poodle you would not be doing the poodle a favor. The poodle—if you were worthy— would be doing one for you. Poodles, it declared, must not be kept outside in doghouses. They also must be properly groomed. This, the author suggested, was something the dog expected of its owners. Were you supposed to believe that those fancy topiary hairstyles had been the dog's idea?

The breeder, according to the short bio, was a German immigrant named Helga, who had immigrated to the United States in the early 1970s, transporting "seventeen poodles on Lufthansa." Her dogs, though nominally French standards, were, she said, of the sturdier and bigger-boned "English" stock.

I began calling Helga in late November of Claire's senior year to inquire about the availability of puppies. I thought a female would be a good match for Pete. What better way to rejuvenate him than with a lively female friend? To my surprise, Helga thought this was a bad idea.

Males, she insisted, were more reliable dogs. "The females are always jumping over the fences and running away," she said. "But the males never do."

Perhaps she was right. Pete, after all, was male and you couldn't wish for a better dog. A young male, sort of an understudy, could be a nice companion. Unless, of course, the younger dog attempted to challenge Pete. Wasn't that what always happened in wolf packs? Weren't the younger ones always looking for an opportunity to overthrow the alpha dog?

I asked our vet about this. He assured me that, in dog relationships, the older dog, even after he had weakened, would remain dominant. "Pete will always be his older brother," he said.

Another month or so went by. Claire had hit a wall in the college-application marathon. She couldn't bear to write one more essay that told why she thought she would be a good match for this or that college, or what life lessons or educational experiences had prepared her for the college "experience."

Everyone was looking for the clever angle, a trick to stand out from the crowd. Claire, having reached the last of these compositional hurdles and run into several dead ends, had decided to write an essay on the difficulty of writing such essays. This trick on herself seemed to work for a while, but it eventually turned into a dead end, too. She'd write a few sentences and then retreat to the family room couch for some time out. I found her asleep there late one night, the computer cursor blinking in the middle of a sentence that began "The computer cursor blinked impatiently, like a teacher tapping her foot . . ."

In the end, she—and we—got through it. The applications were launched, the financial-aid forms were filled out. Now we entered the eye of the storm, the period between the traumatic application process and the traumatic acceptance-rejection period, the period of the fat envelope and the thin envelope.

This seemed like a good time to get the dog, and so, on a snowy February Saturday we all piled into the station wagon for the trip up to Catskill. We brought Pete with us because we'd been advised that it was better to introduce a new puppy to an established dog on the new dog's turf. It was a two-hour drive. We were within view of the Catskill Mountains when we reached our exit. Our directions took us down to the flat plain of the Hudson River.

The big Victorian house looked a little more rundown than it did in the photographs. We parked in the turnaround in front. The snow was falling heavily here. Leaving Pete in the car for the moment, we went up on the porch and rang the bell. Dogs immediately began barking. Lots of dogs. Forty-pound bags of deer food sat on the porch.

Helga, a small woman in her sixties with a thick German accent, greeted us at the door. The house's interior was dark and heavy with woodwork. A grand staircase with a broad banister led to the upstairs. Threadbare oriental rugs were scattered here and there. Helga led us into a large, irregularly shaped parlor. The room looked like one from an English murder mystery. There were doors all around, all of them closed.

"I'll bring the puppies," Helga said, disappearing behind one of the doors. Barking came from all directions. Claire, uncharacteristically bold, strode across the room and opened one. A half-dozen poodles barked at us from several fenced-off alcoves. I recalled what it said on the Web site, about all poodles needing to live in the house—not in outdoor doghouses. An old house this size probably had fifteen rooms. Were there dogs in all of them? Had we wandered into some quirky children's story?

A moment later, a door opened and Helga ushered in about a half-dozen puppies, all shimmying and wagging their tails with excitement. They had been clipped so that they sported Afghan-like mops on their heads. They were ecstatic to be loose and among people. We sat down cross-legged on the rug and let them run among us. They all seemed like wonderful dogs. There were no shy or withdrawn ones. As with Pete, I looked for one who showed a little extra spunk, who was friendly and playful and not too timid or afraid of a little roughhousing. We played with them for about twenty minutes, until we settled on one that everyone liked.

After we made our decision, we asked Helga if it would be all right to bring in Pete. She agreed, although not enthusiastically. Alex and I went out to get him. Walking between the porch and the car, we saw eyes watching us from beneath the boughs of the nearby pine trees. A family of deer stood stock-still, ears erect, apparently waiting for the food on the porch to be served. We put Pete on the leash. He was looking fairly shaggy, certainly far short of the grooming standards spelled out on the Web site. Would we be found unworthy?

"Dat's not a poodle," said Helga after getting one look at Pete. "Dat's a Kerry blue." She was referring to the Kerry blue terrier, a dog whose own peculiar grooming style added a drooping beard to the boxy-shaped head cut.

Luke

I mumbled some excuses about Pete being overdue for a haircut and how we didn't like to clip him too close in the winter. Helga must have needed the money, for she said nothing. We all attended to the more immediate business of the meeting between the two dogs. Pete was straining to get closer to the puppy.

"You better hold onto him," Helga said.

"Oh," I assured her, "Pete's a good dog. He wouldn't do anything, especially to a puppy."

"Vell," she said darkly, "tings happen."

We looked at her.

"Vonce," she said, "a family brought a German shepherd in here to meet the puppy. It bit the puppy on the head. Spilled the brains right onto the rug."

We all stood dumbfounded, our eyes involuntarily drifting down.

I doubled Pete's leash around my hand and let him gradually inch forward. He seemed nothing more than extremely curious. Nor did the puppy shrink in fear from him. Pete wagged his tail, the puppy danced about a bit, and the introductions were complete.

I wrote the check and picked up the puppy, and we headed for the car. The deer were nowhere to be seen now. We put Pete in the rear of the station wagon. The puppy, as yet unnamed, went in the backseat with Claire and Alex. I remember being pleased at what was—for the moment, at least—a new symmetry in the family: two adults, two children, two dogs.

Had I thought about it a little more, I would have realized that, in getting a second dog, I was following a pattern of human behavior that was even better established than the second-child-then-leave-the-city one.

In fact, it was not until I arrived at the vet's office with our puppy that my full motives for getting this dog were pointed out to me. I should add that our vet's son, Luke, was one of Claire's classmates and that both were just a few months shy of graduation.

"Oh," the vet said, after I had lifted the floppy-legged puppy up onto the examination table, "Is this Claire's replacement?"

I think I may have blushed. Honestly, this had never occurred to me. Now I saw it all clearly. I had done exactly what my mother had done when I was also a senior in high school. Megan. My feisty replacement. How could I have forgotten? Was I destined to follow my mother into an embarrassing syndrome, talking to the replacement pet as if it were a child, showering it with attention and concern, putting its diplomas on the wall?

Such insights into one's unconscious motives were supposed to happen in a therapist's office—not a veterinarian's.

A moment later, it was the veterinarian's turn to blush. He asked the puppy's name and I answered the name we had chosen, "Luke." People, even veterinarians, don't like to think that the name they've so lovingly bestowed on a child is the same one that other people think is just right for a dog.

CHAPTER TWENTY-FOUR

Three's a Pack

The two dogs settled into what seemed a congenial relationship, with Luke in the role of the little brother, just as the vet had predicted. What Pete did, Luke did. The transformation was complete when we finally took Luke to the groomer to get rid of Helga's frou-frou haircut. He came back looking like mini-Pete.

There was no need to train or housebreak Luke. He learned everything by imitation. He didn't have Pete's subtle intellect, but he didn't have his stubbornness either. Although they were both black poodles, Pete's was a cooler black, what they call blue, whereas Luke's was a warm, smoky black. He had the same poodle face, but slightly smaller eyes, which made him look a little less soulful than Pete—but also less melancholy. He was trimmer and leggier than Pete, and showed signs of being a fast and graceful runner.

Socially, he had one odd quirk: a fear of small children. He seemed to regard them not as pups of our species but as small, dangerous creatures, like trolls.

It was funny to see him replicate things that Pete had done as a puppy. He looked like our home videos of Pete as he came bursting out of the front door of the house, doing the spin dance on the front lawn. Gradually Pete was regaining some of his former playfulness. He would get a stick, challenge Luke to take it away from him, and soon they were playing those dog-invented games, keep-away and tug-of-war.

Out on the walk, there was a jolly aspect to being three. We weren't just a man and his dog anymore, but a pack. Twice a day we rolled past the old brick factories, went bump-bump over the railroad tracks, and pulled into that small semicircular parking lot, that Outpost-like fortification of boulders and creosoted logs that positioned us between the landscape's two poles, the pastoral and the savage. Some days the dogs and I took to the docile, rolling meadow with its flocks of grazing geese and wide-open sky. Other days we parted the willow trees' weepy branches and slipped into the dense, jungle-like wild with its twisty paths, meandering streams, and wild-animal sightings.

Sometimes the two dogs made me feel the odd man out. Dog trainers like to remind us that dogs are "pack animals." What gets said less often is that humans are too. That is why Pete had fit so well into the pack we called our family. It wasn't a perfect fit, because, of course, Pete was a different species. He was the odd member, the only one on all fours in a pack of uprights. Now, out on the walks, I was the odd member, the human in a dog pack, the only one on two legs. They shared dog scents and dog perceptions that I knew nothing about. They ran in tandem down the Meadowlands road, like the two wolves in the Natural History Museum diorama. They chased rabbits together and confronted other dogs as a more formidable pair.

Often the effect of being alone on my side of the species divide was to revert deeper into my human identity. I had more time to think about things. I started carrying a notebook and writing down what I saw. I studied nature, mulled over books I was reading, wondered about the puzzle called the Meadowlands, and composed art reviews.

The latest work of genius I'd been called upon to review was a . . . shit machine. Literally. It wasn't called that, but that was its function—to produce bowel movements. Some artist had consulted with chemists and biologists and put together this goofy contraption. It looked like a Rube Goldberg device: a funnel at one end and a conveyer belt at the other, with all these mashers, grinders, gurgling bottles, and yards of glass pipe in the middle. Every day, attendants at a Soho museum poured food into its funnel. The contraption chewed it, digested it in various acids, and four hours later delivered a turd down its conveyor belt. It wasn't enough that I had dog crap to deal with. Now the art was crapping, too.

Of course, such subjects presented opportunities for humor and irony. But the art was already ironic, and piling irony on top of irony gets tiresome. In the end, it was one of those assignments that made you wonder what you were doing with your life, and whether, perhaps, you ought to look for more rewarding subjects on which to write.

I still enjoyed writing about Rubens, Rembrandt, Matisse, Ancient Egypt—the art history part of the job—but I had no patience for art that was about process, semiotics, post-structuralism, or shocking the bourgeoisie. The art of our time had turned into a species of mannerism—an art that was always winking at itself.

I felt like I was juggling two very different kinds of wildness. There was the newly discovered wildness of the Meadowlands. This was my dog's world. And there was the wildness of the contemporary art world. That was the art critic's world. One was sincere and restorative. The other was ironic and exasperating.

In time, I found a way to bridge the divide. I convinced my editors to let me try out a new idea for a column: I would write about things in the everyday world from an art critic's perspective. Some of my subjects came straight from the world of dog walking—meadows, harvest moons, trees, ladybugs. But even things encountered elsewhere—the forgotten phone booth, an ocean liner backing into the Hudson River, vending machines—were informed by the habits of observation that I had developed on the dog-walking trail.

CHAPTER TWENTY-FIVE

Deep Sighs and Other Preliminaries

One night, slouched in my oversized reading chair, I glanced up to see two sets of eyes—dark, luminous eyes filled with expectation—staring at me. The faces were alert, filled with hope. They looked at me the way a drought-afflicted farmer stares at the horizon, the way a nervous commuter stares down the empty tracks.

Pete had been staring at me like this for ten years, but with the addition of a second dog, I had begun to feel a much more palpable . . . pressure.

If my dogs were to lodge one complaint against me, it would be my unpredictability. I never neglected to take them out. But I rarely took them at the same time two days in a row. Sometimes I wrote first, sometimes after. At night, I might walk them any time from 7:30 to midnight.

This drove them crazy.

I looked at my watch. It was nearly 10:30.

"Okay," I said, closing my book and uttering the words from which there was no turning back: "Let's go for a walk."

Feet madly scrambled, collars jangled. The two dogs rose to their feet like marionettes jerked up by their strings. They were wildly excited. But their celebration was tinged with anxiety. They knew that things could still go wrong. Having a writer for a companion had given them a lot of long interesting walks, but it also exposed them to the whims and neuroses of someone who could be erratic, hesitant, and absentminded.

Never were my dogs and I more tightly linked—and comically mismatched—than during this getting-out-the-door business. They were the forward momentum. I was the complications.

On this night, I first had to fetch my keys from the bedroom bureau. Eight feet joined my two as we trampled up, then down, the uncarpeted stairs. On the main floor, my escorts tried to herd me in the direction of the front door, but I wanted my pen and notebook from my basement office. This detour generated outright panic. To them, the basement office was the black hole of walking hopes. They threw desperate body blocks to keep me from reaching the stairs. They knew that, once down there, I could drift toward the glowing screen and sit there, tapping my fingers or scribbling something on a yellow pad—and still be scribbling twenty minutes later.

Not tonight. I quickly pocketed notebook and pen and started back up. As we approached the front hall, the launching area, the excitement level went off the scale. I was being drawn into a violent chemical reaction that was about to propel me out the door with the speed of expanding gas.

Despite their reputation for living in the present moment, I had observed that dogs dwelled a lot on the future. Perhaps this was due to their very precise internal clock. According to veterinarian Bruce Fogle in *The Dog's Mind,* dogs trained to do something at a particular time in a 24-hour cycle would hit that time within one minute, day after day.

Amazing. I couldn't be more different from my dogs in this respect. I kept irregular hours. I sometimes stayed up all night. I overslept. I was late for appointments. Meanwhile, my dogs, who had no appointments, no social calendar, no meetings, no jobs— were paragons of punctuality! Within the minute!

In *The Hidden Life of Dogs,* Elizabeth Marshall Thomas entertained a variation on a classic Freudian question. "What," she asked, "do dogs want?" She then set out to get to the bottom of this question and spent—by her own account—more than 100,000 hours observing her three dogs.

I have often marveled over this. Perhaps I am missing something. Perhaps her dogs were of some rare breed that I am unfamiliar with. Cats can be inscrutable, cats contain mysteries, but not dogs. On any given evening, I had only to look at their expectant faces to know what they wanted.

Where Thomas could have helped was in telling them—and me, for that matter—what it was that *I* wanted. Why was I forever hesitating and doubling back from the threshold for one thing or another? Why was I so wrapped up in these myriad objects and accessories and unsure as to which I needed: my wallet, gloves, hat, leashes, binoculars, cell phone, car keys, apple, dog treats, letters to mail, prescriptions to drop at the pharmacy, library books to drop in the library's book-return slot?

I was so absentminded that I once drove to North's house to pick him up for a dog walk only to have it pointed out to me that there were no dogs in the back of the station wagon. How the dogs let me get out that morning, I'll never know. Where was their vigilance when I needed it?

Not an evening went by where they didn't stake me out. They were like two cops: an old veteran and a rookie. They watched my every move, listened to every utterance, pinned their hopes on the slenderest signs. If one got thirsty, his partner covered for him while he went to the toilet for a drink.

This, before anyone thinks me cruel, had nothing to do with biological needs. These animals had access to the backyard on demand. No, this was not about that. This was about *the walk*.

A better dog walker might have settled on a formal routine— got them off their tenterhooks. But whenever I started to feel sorry for them, I'd think: *What else do they have to do? What would they be doing if they weren't watching me?* They didn't read, watch TV, listen to music, talk on the phone, do crossword puzzles, play the cello, or learn foreign languages. What they did read, watch, and puzzle over was *me*.

Part of what makes dogs so appealing is their ability to read the moods and expressions of humans. Less frequently noted is the marvelous human ability to read the expressions and body language of dogs. It sometimes happened, for example, that I would inadvertently give a sign that I was ready to go on the walk. I'd clumsily utter the word "walk" or "out" aloud. Or simply move in the general direction of the front door of the house. If, having given such a signal, I failed to follow through, my dogs sank into despair. They collapsed to the floor and exhaled in exasperation.

"Those sighs of a dog!" wrote British novelist John Galsworthy. "They go to the heart so much more deeply than the sighs of our own kind because they are so utterly unintended, regardless of effect, emerging from one who, heaving them, knows not that they have escaped him!"

Those sighs! Those hangdog expressions! The crestfallen look of a dog that is being left behind! Like Galsworthy, most people saw these emotional displays as "utterly unintended."

And yet, when I thought about it, everything my dogs did—the pleading eyes, the little whimpers, the sad demeanor—pricked my conscience, made me feel guilty, and furthered the dogs' cause.

Even Charles Darwin was taken in. In *The Expression of the Emotions in Man and Animals,* Darwin described his dog's disappointment over his detours to the greenhouse. When he set out from the house, Darwin wrote, the dog would think they were going for a walk and would trot ahead in a state of pleased excitement—head raised, ears up, tail aloft. As soon as Darwin veered off toward the greenhouse to check on his plant experiments, however, the dog's demeanor would collapse.

"His look of dejection was known to every member of the family, and was called his 'hothouse face,'" Darwin wrote. "This consisted in the head drooping much, the whole body sinking a little and remaining motionless; the ears and tail falling suddenly down, but the tail was by no means wagged. With the falling of the ears and of his great chaps, the eyes became much changed in appearance, and I fancied that they looked less bright. His aspect was that of piteous, hopeless dejection; and it was, as I have said, laughable, as the cause was so slight."

What's ironic about this story is that Darwin never invokes a Darwinian explanation. It might have been observed that, without the ability to communicate its feelings so dramatically—even theatrically—the dog wouldn't have won a central place in Darwin's family in the first place. In fact, what was more remarkable than the dog's behavior was that of the people: the Darwin family was so attuned to the dog's emotional life that they all knew what the dog wanted when he made the "hothouse face" and how he felt about not getting it. Whatever the outcome of this particular exchange, was there any doubt that the dog was the winner in the long run because of this?

CHAPTER TWENTY-SIX

The Grassy Strip

The world can sometimes be like a funhouse mirror, reflecting your inner life in a distorted, cartoonish way. So it was one January afternoon, when Janet handed me the newspaper and pointed to a story.

"Did you see this?"

The item was below the fold, on the left side, where editors put quirky human-interest stories.

The headline read: LEGAL MINDS PONDER THE STATUS OF DOG DOO. And below that: WHERE IT IS MAKES ALL THE DIFFERENCE.

I looked at Janet, whose ambivalent smile told me that the story was amusing, but that it might not amuse me so much.

The story concerned a dog walker from our town, whose dog had pooped on the narrow grass strip between the sidewalk and the curb. The dog walker had picked it up in a plastic baggie and was about to carry it away to a trash can when the angry homeowner, a man named William Grappa, confronted him. He insisted that the dog owner—an oboist named Earl Holloway—needed his permission to use the grassy strip whether he picked it up or not. Holloway, under attack, showed the fire that can lurk below an oboist's placid exterior. Words were exchanged.

I pictured this tableau of suburban life: Two men yelling at each other on a tree-lined street; one, red-faced and emotional, pointing down at a thin strip of grass, and the other, jaw set, eyes narrowed, holding a plastic bag full of dog feces. Between them, looking back and forth, the good-natured dog.

A policeman was called. He listened, a little bewildered, as the two sides presented their arguments. When it was over, to Holloway's surprise, he was holding a summons. The wording of the town ordinance did in fact prohibit the unauthorized deposit of dog waste on "private property." What was unclear, and would have to be decided by a judge, was whether the little grassy strip was public or private property.

Friends rallied in support of Holloway. One, standing up at a town council meeting, called the case "an assault" on dog walkers. Holloway, principled and civic-minded, saw serious implications for the fraternity of the leash and the collar. Facing a date with a municipal judge, he said: "If he rules against me, it effectively outlaws dog walking in this town."

"I'm surprised I haven't heard anything about this," I said.

"Well, you're out in the Meadowlands all the time," said Janet. "The only dog walker you talk to is that Joe character, and he doesn't even live in this town."

That was true. But it wasn't just the failure of gossip to reach me that made it so odd. It was the whole thing. By this time, I had already started gathering material for a book about dog walking and was beginning to think of myself as something of an authority on the subject, perhaps a future spokesman for dog walkers. It seemed a sufficiently offbeat preoccupation, such a narrow specialization, that I didn't expect any company or competition, especially from someone in my own tiny town. Up on the bulletin board next to my desk was a quote from Emerson: ". . . no kernel of nourishing corn can come to him but through his toil bestowed on that plot of ground which is given to him to till."

So, what was Earl Holloway doing on my modest little plot? Hadn't he already been given an oboe to toil on? Who was he to rally the dog-walking faithful?

"I don't understand," Janet said. "How can the grassy strip be private property?"

"What?" I said, lost in these reflections.

"The grassy strip," she said. "If that's private property, then the sidewalk, which is even closer to the house, must be private property, too."

I nodded. I knew the grassy strip as well as any suburban dog walker. How many hours had I spent loitering in its vicinity while Pete conducted his olfactory communications? Its constantly unfurling surface was a canine community message board.

Homeowners, however, weren't exactly in love with this odd little piece of land. It was hard to get a lawn mower in there. Unruly tufts of grass required edging or hand trimming. It was a magnet for litter and debris.

"They can't be serious about this permission business," I said. "Are people supposed to go around getting waivers from all their neighbors?"

"It sounds like a Monty Python skit."

"Yes," I said, "The Department of Silly Dogwalks."

Janet got up to put on hot water.

"This poor Holloway, though," she said. "He says in the story that he's spent $800 in legal expenses, so far."

"I don't know about 'poor Holloway,'" I said.

"What do you mean?"

"He seems a little melodramatic. All that 'end of dog walking' business."

"He didn't say 'end of dog walking,'" said Janet. "He was just saying what you were saying—that if people were going to have to get permission for their dogs to go on the grassy strip, then—" she picked up the story and scanned for the quote—"*'then, it will effectively outlaw dog walking in this town.'*"

"Give me liberty or give me death!" I said.

"Why are you being so sarcastic?"

"I'm not being sarcastic," I said.

"Well, suppose it had happened to you?"

"That's why I go to the Meadowlands," I said. "I found that it took some of the poetry out of the experience when you had to pick up the crap in a bag. And then, because the public trash baskets are only on the main streets, you have to bring it home and put it in your own trash—"

"Really, it's not that bad."

"Not the way you do it," I said. "You just throw the bag straight into the garbage can where the garbage men ignore it, so these little bags accumulate in the bottom, and there's always an inch or two of water down there because the raccoon chewed a hole in the lid and the whole mess—"

"Oh stop. Just stop."

"But think about it," I said. "What is the point of walking all the way around the block if the bag ends up three feet from the back door and I have to clean it up?"

"Please."

We each sipped the tea Janet had made.

"Well, you're going to support him, aren't you?" asked Janet. "I mean you, of all people."

"Support him how?" I said. "Are they going to dog-walk on Washington?"

"I think it said something about a fund-raiser for his legal bills," said Janet.

"Oh, I don't know," I said. "I'm a private dog walker. Anyway, do you actually think they're going to ban dog walking?"

"I don't know. Well, what do you think he should do?"

"I think he should walk his dog in the dump like a normal person."

That night, I took Pete and Luke down to the town ball fields. Lately, this had become our after-dark place. I would have preferred to be in the park meadow. The problem was Joe. Every once in a while, the park police came by and kicked us out. Sometimes they threatened to ticket us. At that point, our course of action was clear to me. We should leave. Joe, however, didn't believe in graceful retreats. He kept insisting that the park police who enforced the curfew were actually just nighttime security guards with no real legal authority.

I had no idea if this were true or not, but Joe's attitude was that we should defy them. When they told him he'd have to leave, he'd curse and yell with surprising vehemence. I would edge away from him at such moments just in case he was wrong and these officers did have the power to arrest or ticket us. The fines for these things—unleashed dogs, using the park after sundown—could run into the hundreds of dollars.

There was always this side to dog walking. Even if you did everything right, like Mr. Holloway, you could get in trouble. Usually, it came down to a fight over land. Dogs reconnected you with the land, but in the process, they often ignored or trampled on all these fussy human boundaries and regulations, whether it was flower borders, the grassy strip, park curfews, or leash laws. In New York City, fights over park leash laws had been going on since the mid-1980s—especially in the big Olmsted parks of Central Park in Manhattan and Prospect Park in Brooklyn, where the convincing naturalism made people yearn for a more natural experience for their dogs.

I parked in my usual place—at the back of the pool parking lot. Instead of crossing the tracks, however, as the dogs and I did when we went into the Meadowlands, we cut behind the next-door synagogue to the ball fields. First, though, the dogs took care of business in the adjacent DPW dumping area. Lately, a heap of chopped-up Christmas trees gave the place a pleasant evergreen scent.

With that out of the way, we walked over to the fields and slipped through a tall hedgerow. I loved the transition from the starkly lit parking lot to the dark field. The dogs disappeared like phantoms into the darkness, and the night sky slid into view overhead as if a roof had been rolled back. For a while I occupied myself scanning the sky for constellations. I had gotten a field guide to "The Night Sky" for this purpose, but I hadn't gotten very far with it. Our light pollution, which renders our night sky ultramarine instead of black, was supposed to make constellation hunting easier—it made the fainter, and therefore irrelevant, stars invisible. Still I couldn't find most of these fanciful constructs. All I'd learned so far was to add a few details to the few constellations I already knew. Instead of just Orion's belt, for example, I had learned to see his shoulders and one foot. He still didn't have a head, but that wasn't my fault—there was no head, apparently—which is the sort of leap of faith that constellation hunting is always demanding of you.

Nevertheless, I always took solace in the night sky because here, I told myself, was something eternally wild. The sky I looked up at wasn't so very different from the one my Paleolithic ancestors took in—even if I couldn't quite see it as clearly as they had. What could be wilder—a purer expression of uncorrupted nature—than the stars, the planets, the face of the moon? Tonight my eyes were drawn to just such a presence shimmering in the western sky. Was this Venus? I couldn't remember if Venus was a "morning star" or an "evening star" or both. As I debated this, and wondered whether it was supposed to be in that part of the sky, the bright blip bulged on one side and spawned a second blip. Oh, wait. This was no planet or star, but an airplane! A commercial jet had been flying straight at me, headlights blazing so brightly that they had fused into one light. As it banked, red and green wing-lights twinkling, it fell into line behind two other planes. They were in the southbound corridor to Newark Airport. So much for star-gazing in North Jersey.

But this was one of those head-clearing dog walks. By the time I finished three circuits and had rounded up the near-invisible Pete and Luke, all thoughts of grassy strips, curfews, outlawed dog walking, and dog-walker usurpers had evaporated.

North called the next morning.

"Are we walkin'?" he asked.

I said we were.

"Did you see it on TV last night?"

"See what?"

"About the dog walker. It was on the news."

"No," I said.

"It was on CNN," he said.

"You're kidding."

After North and I hung up, I gathered up coat and leashes and headed out. It was a bright, sunny day. Luke flew out of the house like a cannonball, and Pete bounced after like a loose bowling ball. We were into the car and off, weaving down the twisty streets of North's Victorian neighborhood. North was already out on the sidewalk when we pulled up. My promiscuous poodles gave him the big greeting, yipping and whimpering excitedly as if he were St. Francis.

"It's not you they love," I said.

"Yes, I know, it's the walk," he said as he climbed in.

"Purely Pavlovian," I said.

We drove first to the Korean convenience store. Inside, North thumbed through the tabloids and found an AP version of the grassy-strip story under the headline MUCH ADOO-DOO ABOUT NOTHING!

"The headline writers are having a ball," I said.

"Did you know we had three hundred ninety-seven dogs in town?" North asked when we got back into the car.

"Does that sound like a lot?"

"It's almost as many kids as there are in the middle school," North said.

"There do seem to be a lot more dog walkers around than there used to be," I said.

We sipped our coffees. The dogs had wolfed down their rolls and were staring at the backs of our heads, hoping for another handout.

"So, where do you stand on this grassy strip?" North asked. "No pun intended."

"I stand with the dogs," I said. "I think they're entitled to their skinny little piece of land. It's part of the public right-of-way, isn't it?"

"I guess," said North. "But if the sidewalk and the strip are public, why did I have to pay $2,000 to put in new sidewalks?"

This was a question that rankled people in the suburbs. In the city, no one ever questioned the communal use of the sidewalk. Here in the suburbs, however, people were testier about property rights. They saw an inherent contradiction in having to pay for and be liable for something that was dedicated for public use.

"Anyway," said North, as we headed toward the Meadowlands. "Let's get to the important issue. Have you met your doppelganger?"

"My what?"

"Your doppelganger. Your dog-walking double."

"Holloway?"

"Yes, are you acquainted?"

"No," I said. "Does he look like me?"

"Don't be so literal," said North. "He's assumed your mantle."

"Oh, come on."

"He's become the number-one dog walker in the country. You watch, he'll be on *Oprah*."

Now I had to laugh. North, in one of his more expansive speculations, had already booked *us* on *Oprah*—Mr. Dog Walker and his quotable sidekick.

"I think you're the doppelganger," I said. "Come on, let's get to the Meadowlands."

Win or lose, the grassy-strip controversy had empowered the town's dog-walking community. The case had given them all the ingredients of a revolution: a common oppressor (Grappa!), a martyr (Hollowell!), and contested land (The Grassy Strip!). They had shed the characteristic dog-walker deference and inferiority complex that comes from the negative messages society is always sending ("No dogs allowed!" "Leash your dog!" "Pick up after your dog!"). The dog walkers had become a political constituency in town just like the Sports Boosters, The Seniors, and the Taxpayers' Association. They would be heard!

The court case dragged on for months with various postponements and delays. I, for one, forgot about it—until I saw this headline on our front page:

JUDGE SAYS CURBS ARE OFF-LIMITS TO DOGS
SIDEWALK, GRASS STRIP, EVEN STREET ARE PRIVATE PROPERTY

As North says, the law is an ass. The judge had reached into centuries-old English common law to dig himself into this hole. Holloway was said to have "barked" his protest outside the courthouse. Town officials were described as doing lots of "soul searching as well as sole searching."

It took a full year, from the date of the alleged crime to the reversal by a Superior Court judge, to clear Holloway of wrongdoing. The upper court's decision reestablished the right of town dog walkers to make use of the sidewalk, grassy strip, and gutter—as long as they cleaned up after their dogs.

Meanwhile, the newly empowered dog walkers were no longer content with the grassy-strip diaspora. They wanted true land reform. They wanted a dog park.

And they got it. The town council, perhaps weary of the town being made a laughingstock in scatological headlines, gave the group half of a little-used park at the north end of town. It wasn't much land—maybe the size of an urban playground, but it was viewed as a great victory. Of course, the non-dog-owning neighbors immediately protested this confiscation of parkland that had, they tearfully told the council, once belonged to their children.

Their protest—angry signs on their front lawns, petitions to the council, denunciations of the dog people on the community Listserv—continues to this day.

Meanwhile, the park proved immensely popular and drew many of the town's 397 dogs and their owners. People loved it. They made friends. The dogs made friends. When I drove by, I would see them all in there, the people standing around the two big picnic tables drinking coffee and schmoozing, and the dogs circulating in a noisy pack.

It was a great social experience for everybody. And for the dogs, it was a great physical outlet. Many of them were getting more exercise than they had gotten in the pre–dog park days when they were walked on a leash.

For the people, however, the opposite was often true. Unless they made a special effort to walk to and from the park rather than driving (which, when combined with the time spent in the dog park, was more time than most people could spare), they barely walked at all. Belonging to the dog park turned out to be an extremely passive form of recreation. Little muscle exertion was required. Few calories were burned. One woman who had a middle-aged dog was heard to remark that since joining the dog park her dog had lost five pounds and she had gained ten.

So, The Grassy-Strip Case had a paradoxical outcome. Dog walking had not been "outlawed" in our town, as feared. But for many, it had become, well, superfluous.

CHAPTER TWENTY-SEVEN

Seeing the Clubhouse

We walked in a line, the three of us, arrayed on the Meadowlands road: Luke in front, me in the middle, and Pete bringing up the rear. We were like the dog-walking version of that great old painting by Titian, *Three Ages of Man,* but instead of the angelic babes, the two handsome lovers, and the feeble old man, this one featured a young dog, a middle-aged man, and a feeble old dog.

We were on a time line of sorts, arranged not by absolute years lived, or even by life expectancy, but by level of vitality. Luke, in the lead, had so much bounce in his step that his feet barely touched the ground. I strode along, holding my own. But Pete trudged so heavily that his feet barely left the ground. He sloshed through every puddle like some weary wildebeest at the end of the great migration.

One of Claire's dates took in his droopy demeanor and nick-named him "Eeyore."

Hearing this was a little arrow in all our hearts. *Eeyore? Pete? Our Pete? That sad donkey from Winnie the Pooh?*

Why, he was only—what—fourteen?—the age of a human ado-lescent. I once held him in my arms, a young pup, but by the cruel trick of dog years, he had passed me. His eyes conveyed sorrows of agedness that I had yet to endure.

The three-slot processional order that the dogs and I settled into was, I discovered, unalterable. It didn't matter if I slowed down to let Pete catch up, or called Luke back and got everyone in a bunch, or walked more slowly, or more quickly. The pattern prevailed. Pete, I finally figured, hung back out of an old dog's craftiness: he didn't want to take unnecessary steps. Back there, he could keep an eye on me. If I stopped, he stopped. He watched me. If I headed up to the Rock Pile, which he knew was a dead end, he would flop down on the ground and wait for Luke and me to return.

Our sometimes-companion North was on the same wavelength lately. "I feel old," he announced one day, out of the blue. He didn't say it with self-pity. Well, maybe a little self-pity. But he seemed more surprised than anything by this trick of time, that he, North, just yesterday a newly minted college graduate driving a new Volvo through Europe, could have become this late-middle-aged man with a paunch and a bald pate. "I can see the clubhouse," he said, squinting into the distance.

Coincidentally, our walks took us past the county horseback riding center, so there really *was* a clubhouse, and I could see it, too. But I knew what he meant, though he was barely sixty, not really old by today's standards, and in good health. Nowadays there were men in their sixties with Charles Atlas builds, hair transplants, and trophy wives.

There were also those at the other end of the bell curve, the ones picked off early, friends who succumbed to cancer, heart attacks, unfortunate falls. For nearly one whole year of dog walking, I listened to North chronicle the slow death from cancer of his childhood friend. This friend got up one morning, stood in front of the bathroom mirror, and noticed something on the white of his eye, like a freckle where a freckle shouldn't be. A melanoma.

The doctors cut it out but let him keep his eye, a miscalculation. They later took the eye anyway, then the surrounding musculature and a good part of one side of his face, while tumors in his body cavity swelled so large they broke ribs. It was horrific. North's friend was rich, an heir to an advertising fortune, and so, his demise had a glaze of gothic grandeur. Most of us have been led to believe that hospital rooms, like voting booths, are the same for everyone, but North's friend, for whatever comfort it gave him, was on a floor in Sloan Kettering that North said "looked like one in the Plaza Hotel."

North, a loyal friend, went every Sunday to sit and comfort and reminisce, and then Monday or Tuesday morning he would join us on the dog-walking trail, where, at the first lull in the conversation, he would say, "I saw my friend Mark, yesterday . . ." and there would follow the whole gruesome report. And being North's loyal friend, as North was to Mark, I did my slighter duty, which was to let him shed a little grief in my direction.

After a while, I admit, I found myself wishing that his friend would die and put an end to all this. Between Pete's decrepitude and North's deathbed vigil, our walks were getting too crowded with *memento mori*—reminders of death. Old Masters often put one in a still-life painting or a portrait so that viewers wouldn't forget that life was just a vale of tears. We were like a painting that had both a skull and a turned-over hourglass.

On the nice days, Pete still smiled up into the sunshine. He still enjoyed a soak in the creek. But getting him to the Meadowlands had new challenges. Some nights if it was too cold, or too late, he needed to be cajoled into going. I'd say what used to be the magic word—"walk"—and he would just stare at me from his dog bed by the fireplace.

He could no longer jump into the back of the station wagon, so he and I worked out a method for getting him up. He'd put his front paws up on the tailgate, then turn to me to signal that he was ready. I'd reach down and take hold of both of his back legs and lift. In he'd go.

We got it down pat, like a circus trick. It always amused friends to see this little routine of ours. They'd shake their heads and chuckle at the oh-so-human way Pete looked over his shoulder, patiently awaiting my assistance. I tried to be jaunty about it. I made jokes about being Pete's obedient footman. *Into the carriage now, your lordship.* But in truth, I was trying not to see his sad expression. I couldn't blame him. He used to sail up into the back of the station wagon, to literally jump so high in getting in that he would be on a descending arc when he landed.

Luke and Pete looked less and less like twins. Pete had the old dog's physique, skinny legs on a barrel-shaped body. Luke, long legged and slender, had the cut of a thoroughbred. Sometimes on nighttime walks in the ball fields, Luke would get a little too spirited and knock Pete over with a body bump. I'd yell at the aggressor and try to comfort Pete for this humiliation, but I sensed that neither animal understood my complaint. The problem was, dogs accept this pack behavior. If Pete were a wolf, and the leader of a pack, and he became old, a young wolf like Luke would challenge him. They would fight, the young wolf would win, and the old one would slink off and become a lone wolf. When he was unable to get enough food as a solitary hunter, he would die. No wolf in the wild would ever get to the point of decrepitude that Petey had reached. Old age is another of the human life experiences that we had bestowed on our friend, the dog.

An additional sad thing about old age—for animals and humans, alike—was that the aged one sometimes became a little ridiculous. Pete had become the family crackpot. As much as we loved him, we couldn't help sometimes laughing at his behavior. All his movements were abrupt, overly emphatic. We'd pet him, and his head would pop up in a sudden jerk. He had trouble getting to his feet. Sometimes, at night, I'd hear him scrambling around, slipping on the hardwood floors trying to get his feet underneath him. And if you tried to help him, he'd just collapse back in a heap as if to say, "Oh, it's hopeless. You do something about this."

Sometimes, I lost patience with him. He had to be nudged to go down the stairs. And the nudge often turned to a push, and sometimes a slap on the butt to get him moving. I told myself it was just like the little slap horseback riders sometimes gave their steeds, or what a shepherd did to his sheep, but horses and sheep weren't capable of all those theatrically sad or guilty faces that dogs made. After he was gone, I'd think, I would regret each of those little rump slaps.

Eventually Pete not only had to be lifted into the back of the station wagon, he had to be lifted out of it. He was afraid to jump down. He'd move to the edge of the station wagon gate and peer down, his head swinging back and forth like a bobble-head doll.

I read an article in the paper that said old people live with the constant fear of falling. They're afraid they'll break a hip. It's a legitimate fear. How often did you hear that someone broke a hip, went into a decline, and died? So, according to this article, they begin to think more and more about it, until the fear of falling becomes a risk itself, like a crippling phobia. I saw it with my mother, a caution so excessive that no movements were natural. Everything—the act of stepping onto a curb, or around a puddle, became so self-conscious that it made a fall more likely. When we walked, I felt her bony hand hooked around the inside of my arm, squeezing, kneading almost, in little spasms of fear or worry.

I saw the same worry in Pete's eyes as he stood looking over the edge of the station wagon tailgate. He had become progressively more cautious. Beyond a certain point he wouldn't jump, couldn't make himself jump. He leaned out and stared at the ground, got a fix on it, measured, looked again, and waggled his mangy old head. Then he looked up at me, and catching my impatient stare, blinked and averted his eyes guiltily. He'd inch forward in order to get his back legs on the lower lip of the tailgate, reducing the jump by a couple of inches, and sometimes those two inches were the difference, and he'd leap.

Other times, I had to lift him down. I was glad to do it. But he hated that, too. He had no trouble accepting assistance in getting *in*to the car, but this, for some reason, felt out-of-control to him. Sometimes it was a real struggle. He'd hang back and I'd have to lean into the back of the Buick's cavernous space—a real stretch. I'd grab him, he'd lean all his weight back, and I'd pull—worried now about my own back. It was an awkward maneuver, leaning forward like that, not the way you were supposed to lift things if you were prone to disc problems. You were supposed to keep heavy weights close to your body and I was leaning forward, yanking on this resistant weight, doing all the wrong things. I really shouldn't be doing this, I'd tell myself, which, I guess is what Pete was telling *himself.*

But what was I going to do? Leave him in there? We'd tried everything. For a while we used a special dog ramp made for this very purpose. It was carpeted for traction and had low side rails that I guess were supposed to make the dog feel more secure. It weighed a ton and was a nuisance sliding in and out of place. I half knew that Pete wouldn't walk on it as soon as I saw it. It was too narrow, in my opinion, and those side rails, I think, had the opposite effect for which they were intended. Instead of making him feel more secure, they made him more leery. They gave it the quality of a chute. It reminded me of the old days, trying to get him to walk on that plank over the canal.

So that went in the attic where the puppy crate had been banished so many years ago.

I remember one night, in particular. Luke was running around in the Grove and Pete was still hanging back in the wagon. We were man and dog, out in the existential landscape, locked in an anxious embrace, each fretting over the threats to his skeletal system, making calculations of impact, pressure, and leverage.

Plus it was cold. And we were in the park after hours. I had an article to finish, my back was already acting up because of all the snow shoveling and ice chipping, it had been a goddamn hard winter, and I was in this grim silent struggle with an animal. I pulled. He pulled. I was trying not to lose my temper, and I didn't want to yank his collar, which I knew was demeaning, but it was hard for me to get a good grip on him. I needed to get under him, lift him a bit, but he was dug in. He had himself into a position, like a good wrestler, where he knew that it would take a lot more of my strength to pull him out than it would take of his to stay put. All the leverage was on his side. And, in his brute animal mind, he knew it.

And Petey, poor old Petey, sensitive to a fault, cringed with self-loathing. How did we get to this place? I was a good owner, a kind owner. I didn't beat my dog. I tried to remind myself of all that I'd learned about dog communication, how dogs had this repertoire of submissive signals that they used to resolve status conflicts in the pack. It was all very stylized, like Kabuki Theater. All this cringing and head hanging were signals they used with one another, and maybe we humans took it too seriously, I'd tell myself. A dog tossed off a few cringes, the way we muttered "excuse me" to a stranger, where what we were really thinking was "watch where you're going, idiot."

But I didn't really believe it. In truth, I could see he was just sick about the whole thing. Finally I had a purchase on him, and I was slowly extracting him, picturing how this would all look to an outsider, like a silent movie of a man struggling with his stubborn mule. I saw it all translated into the crisp, jerky movements of the medium: the pantomime and exaggerated body language, Pete's cringes and furrowed brow, my sighs and foot stompings.

We had done this before. He knew that I wouldn't make him jump. I wouldn't let him topple out like a sack of potatoes. I brought him stiff-legged to the edge, put one arm between his front legs, the other under his belly, and lifted. He was a good seventy pounds. In the air his legs flailed around desperately until he reached the ground.

Sometimes, in the middle of the night he'd bark repeatedly for no apparent reason. I'd come downstairs and he would be sitting there, not barking out the window, not disputing with the cat about something. Just barking. When I asked him what he wanted, he simply looked at me. He wasn't trying to lure me into the kitchen for a treat. He wasn't even bothering to get up. But, like a senile old man, he was muttering to himself, and giving an occasional cry of—what?—existential despair? Was he thinking *My time is drawing near*? Did he, like North, see "the clubhouse in the distance"?

Sometimes, I'd sit down on the floor with him. He'd be tense as a steel cable. I'd try to make him relax and calm down. I'd pet him and scratch him behind the ears, the way he always liked it. I'd talk soothingly to him, and he'd relax a little. Then I could see the old Pete in there, behind those clouded lenses. He'd respond to the gentle scratches around his ears. Emotion would well up. He'd look at me and, just like a person in a dog suit, audibly gulp.

CHAPTER TWENTY-EIGHT

Gates Closing

When you find the right dog-walking place you can become deeply attached to it. You may not even realize how deep that attachment is until someone locks you out. So it was that I drove to the Meadowlands Outpost one day and saw a sign hung on the open gate.

"Overpeck Park South will close on or about October 27 for renovations . . ."

I couldn't believe it. I read it several times. In two weeks, the park would close and would stay closed for more than a year. For what, exactly? The sign gave no clue.

How had I heard nothing about this? How could they close a public park without consulting the public? What needed renovating? The bleachers? The backstops? The tennis courts? By all means. But the park itself? The earth? The creek? The trees? Surely those things were not in need of "renovation."

What could possibly take an entire year?

That night, as I pulled into the parking-lot Outpost, Joe was there, smoking his pipe, as usual.

"What the hell . . . ?" I said to him as I got out of the car.

He shook his head and spit on the ground. I pulled down the tailgate. Luke bounded out and joined a wriggling Mike. Pete came cautiously to the threshold and I quickly snatched him and lowered him to the ground.

"They'll never do it," he said.

I said that they looked pretty serious about doing it.

"They've been talking about this for years," said Joe, who lived in town.

"They have?" I said. "Nobody told me."

"Yeah, well, nothing ever happens. Besides, how are they going to keep us out?"

"There's a gate," I said. "They'll lock it."

"It'll never happen," he said.

Joe was such an outsider, was so distrustful of authority of any kind, that he couldn't distinguish between the trivial harassment of the nighttime park security patrols and a public notice signed by the county parks commissioner. It was all the same "bullshit" to him.

"Even if they lock the gate," Joe said. "All you need is a bolt cutter to make a door in the fence." He gestured toward the length of fence along the ShopRite supermarket lot. "Snip, snip, snip."

I called my friend Gerry, who was mayor of our town. He had seen the plans. He said the park was being turned into "a regional athletic facility" for Little League and high school baseball, football, soccer, and track and field school competitions.

"There are already fields there," I said.

"They want regulation fields," said Gerry. "State of the art. Dugouts. Electronic scoreboards. Astroturf. Stadium seating. Public address systems. Like an Olympic facility."

As Gerry explained it, the county had budgeted for two such facilities—one in the northern end of the county and one at our end. But the northern towns, more rustic in appearance, more upscale, didn't want one of their parks converted into a "facility." So the county parks department doubled the budget on the southern one.

"They didn't want any of the contractors to miss out on these lucrative contracts," said Gerry. "They're big donors to the party and this is their payback."

"Oh great," I said. "What about my meadow?"

"I didn't see any *meadow* on the plans," said Gerry. "I did see a lot of asphalt."

I was furious. I e-mailed one of the reporters at our paper. I complained to everyone I knew. But no one, other than a few fellow dog walkers, seemed to think it much of a big deal. Most suburban people, I noticed, didn't use parks the way their counterparts did in the city. For most middle-class suburbanites, a park was the place you went to watch your kid play organized ball.

It was mostly immigrants new to the area who used the park in a traditional way—for walks, picnics, barbecues, and impromptu games. And the dog walkers.

All of us were, to some degree, disenfranchised. The immigrants were disenfranchised in the way immigrants have always been—they were newcomers who couldn't vote, didn't have political clout, and didn't understand how things were done. They didn't know that the culture expected them to buy houses with decks and big backyards if they wanted to have picnics and barbecues. And that if they or their children wanted to play ball, they should sign up for an organized league.

We dog walkers were disenfranchised because, in the end, despite the advances of dog-inspired land-reform movements, we were still seen as spokespersons for non-human users of the park—animals that ran around on all fours and crapped on the ground. Who were any of us to compete with children in uniforms whose names were being called out on public address systems?

For this, the park's regular users were being pushed off the land? Granted there weren't huge numbers of such people, but there were some—the golfer practicing chip shots, the sunbathing lady in the leopard-print bikini, the man doing Tai Chi, the power walker with the radio headset, the napping limo driver, the scantily clad jogger, the Guatemalan fishermen, the Korean church Bible group, the Ecuadorian soccer players, the miniature powerboat enthusiasts, the father-son kite flyers, the elegant horsewomen, the kids playing home-run derby, the lovers sitting by the river, the sad turbaned man who walked along the river with his hands locked behind his back.

At any random time, there would usually be somebody doing something. But once it was covered with Astroturf and parking-lot asphalt, once they were finished fencing in all the valuable fields and locking their gates, once it became a "sports complex," it would be empty most of the time, just like big stadiums were.

I was surprised at how bereft I felt. How had I ever become so attached to this ordinary piece of land? After all, this wasn't Walden, or Wordsworth's Lake District, or Taos, New Mexico, or even Central Park. This was an uninspired bit of public landscaping on top of a landfill, a place where yellow ShopRite bags blew across the open spaces like tumbleweeds on the prairie and where the hum of the turnpike rivaled the buzz of the insects.

Yet, for the dogs, and for me, big things played out on this modest ground. Here, in the spacious meadow, in the mysterious grove, and on the banks of the ever-rolling creek we had all of creation: sky, wind, clouds, water, moon, trees, grass, birds. What more did Thoreau have?

What was doubly painful about this, I realized, was that no one else really perceived an injustice. I was in the same position as the child who has invested meaning in something, only to watch it be dismantled by adults who haven't a clue what it represents. As far as the park people were concerned, there was nothing *there* to take away. There was only something to be improved.

For the first time in my life I understood in a personal way why people became so passionate about land—why, since the beginning of history, there were fights and wars and bitter struggles over it. It wasn't just about livelihood—the ability to farm or raise animals or even having a place to live. People beat their breasts and fought and died when it would have been easier just to move. It was about attachment.

The dogs and I began the search for a new place. To be uprooted like this, to have to vary our routine, was doubly hard because of Pete's age. I had all I could do to get him in and out of the car. He was like Grandpa Joad in *The Grapes of Wrath*—too old to make the trip.

Well, I thought, the park might be lost to us, but we hadn't lost the wild and the creek. All we had to do was find a new way in. We couldn't walk the plank anymore. Pete was too old for that, although it hardly mattered, because the planks were disappearing too frequently, and I was getting tired of combing the reeds to see where a flood surge—or vandals—had tossed them. We had to find another way in.

I drove down all the dead-end streets in the industrial area that backed up to the Meadowlands. I drove behind factories and stared at chain-link fences. Here and there, I found little gaps where it looked like kids slipped through. I might have fit, but as much as I accepted the ways of the fringe, I couldn't see myself doing that. Not on a daily basis. I turned my attention to the horseback riding center.

The riding center was a place I could never figure out. It was in a county park, and yet it seemed to function as a private riding academy. Wealthy people—many from New York City—kept their horses there. A big gate separated it from the rest of the park. The main buildings—the offices, stables, and a huge indoor riding shed—were set well back behind a stand of oak and willow trees, surrounded by acres of corrals and fenced pasture. The gate had signs warning off "non-equestrians." From a distance, you could sometimes see the riders—always female—their horses prancing around the practice rings.

There were stable hands and lawn mower men and even border collies that patrolled the place. I'm basically a law-abiding person. I didn't like the idea of having to sneak in every day. Once we were chased, once we'd been put on notice, then things could get unpleasant. But I didn't see any choice. I decided that if I stuck near the bushes along the railroad tracks and kept the dogs on leash, we could cut through their property unobtrusively. Once we were on the Meadowlands road, we'd be free.

I went back to the Outpost a few nights before the closing date and found Joe under a waning near-full moon. He was getting ready to go hunting for snow geese—a four-day trip to Quebec. The moon shone off the yellowish-gray hair around the fringe of his trucker hat. He told me the details of the trip. When he was finished I asked him where he was going to walk his dog when he returned.

Joe looked around as if he still couldn't conceive that we could be locked out.

I told him I didn't think I was up for the cut-through-the-fence scenario.

"So where will you go?" he asked me.

I had already told him about the ball fields and the parking behind the town pool, but I gave him the directions, again. Then I told him about the way I found through the riding stables into the Meadowlands.

"There's a dead-end street where you can park and cross over the tracks."

He nodded, but I could tell he wouldn't come. There was too much walking involved at both places. Joe needed a stationary location, like those duck blinds he hunted from.

Gates Closing

"There's that new dog park in my town . . ." I added.

His eyes drifted away again. I had the feeling he would shoot his dog before he would hang around with a group of suburban women drinking lattes. We exchanged phone numbers, and I wished him good luck on his hunting trip. Then I watched as he and Mike drove away in their little pickup.

This other end of the Meadowlands presented a somewhat different experience. Instead of entering by a winding path that took us immediately into the wilderness and around the Water Hole, as we did when we went in through Overpeck South, or by the plank that put us in front of the road up to the Rock Pile as we did from the pool parking lot, we had to trek along the straight road for a half mile or so to reach any paths into the interior. Luke fell into his long-distance wolfish side trot—front and back ends moving at a slight angle to each other. But Pete invariably fell behind, and there were many mornings where he fell so far behind that we'd turn back before reaching the interior. It was a rare day when we made it all the way to the creek.

Pete's downhill slide seemed to be accelerating. He was becoming incontinent in the house and it was getting harder and harder to get him out for walks. He was on steroids now. The vet said it would help the arthritis in his back and give him a little more energy. A half hour or so before it was time to go on the walk, I'd give him the pill wrapped in a chewy treat. When it had taken effect, I'd lure him into the standing position with more treats, and I'd use additional treats to get him out the front door, down the steps, and finally to the back of the car, where I could lift him in. He was getting too old and stiff even for that trick of putting his front legs up.

At night, when we drove to the pool parking lot, I'd back up to the curb in the turnaround—usually scraping my tailpipe in the process—just to give him a slightly more elevated and grassy surface to jump down on. The walks got shorter and shorter.

How far were we from the end? I wondered.

Janet brought it up at dinner on New Year's Eve. She and Claire—who was on break from college—had driven the dogs to the Mystery Trails in Claire's old Volvo sedan. But when they got there, they couldn't get Petey out of the car.

"I think we have to think about . . . well, you know . . ." Janet said.

I said no, that I wasn't ready for that. I tried to picture myself taking Pete to the vet for euthanasia. Dog lovers who did this nowadays always described going in with their dogs and holding them while the dog received the lethal injection. I couldn't imagine it. I didn't even want to think about it.

Some weeks went by and one night, going into the library, I saw an announcement on the bulletin board for a meeting about a place called the "Overpeck Preserve." I read with curiosity, wondering where this place was—until I realized it was a name someone had given to the Meadowlands we walked in.

Apparently a committee had been formed to come up with "a plan" for my marsh-turned-landfill-turned-forgotten-fringe-area-wilderness. I felt like an army was advancing, taking first the park, and now setting its sights on the wilderness territory.

Still, it wasn't a complete surprise. Change was coming to the Meadowlands—or at least grandiose plans for change—many of which had been featured on the front page of our paper. Most of the plans were for the Route 3 corridor near Giants Stadium. There were so many plans and they were always being modified or handed off to some new developer that it was hard to keep them all straight or to know which ones to take seriously. There were proposals out there for a country-club community with hotels and golf courses, another for a recreational area of ball fields and picnic groves that would be the size of "ten Central parks," another for a shopping mall and indoor amusement park complex.

In the midst of all this came a proposal for a minor league baseball stadium up at our end, in my very Meadowlands. Most of the community rose up to denounce the plan, citing the increased traffic that it would bring. The plan then hopscotched across the creek to another town's piece of the Meadowlands, where it ran into other problems and then fell dormant.

But the baseball stadium fiasco had awakened interest in the local Meadowlands. What was to be done with it? A couple of the other towns along the creek were suing the county to make good on half-century-old promises to make their land into parks after the dumps were capped.

The meeting was in the basement of the library. The room was nearly full. I recognized many of those in attendance, although, over eight years, I had never seen a single one of them in the Meadowlands. I found a seat. Leading the meeting was a local sculptor named Gil Hawkins. He had grown up in town, a product of the town's Golden Age. His father had been a painter and illustrator and his mother had written books on food and cooking. Gil made abstract aluminum sculptures, several of which stood on people's lawns around town.

He and his group, I was grateful to hear, favored something natural rather than recreational. Soon they were talking about woodchip-covered trails, bridges and boardwalks, maybe wildlife-viewing platforms. The trails, it was said, could be laid out so as to double as a cross-country course for the high school team.

But the centerpiece of this plan, the thing that seemed to make everyone gush with pride was the "interpretive center." A colored drawing on an easel showed a pseudo-rustic building set against some trees. The scene didn't look anything like the Meadowlands. It would be built at the top of the Rock Pile and would have to be automobile accessible, so as to meet requirements for the handicapped.

I tried to picture vans and school buses driving up the Meadowlands road to an asphalt parking lot on top of the Rock Pile. The more they talked, the more it became clear that they weren't going to preserve the place so much as remake it.

They would contain the strata of garbage along the riverbank by covering it with rocks. That seemed like a good idea. But then they started talking about "remediation"—bringing in dirt to build up the cap over the trash. This would necessitate replanting, but that would all be for the good, it was said, because the replacements would be "native species."

I left the meeting dejected. I had tried, in a fairly inarticulate way, to make a pitch for what Thoreau called "absolute freedom and wildness," which even Thoreau admitted was "an extreme statement"—and that was in the 1850s. Nowadays, it was beyond extreme. No one really had a clue as to what I was talking about. They were offended at any suggestion that they refrain from putting a building in there. It was like telling the church committee not to build the church.

I knew that my own vision of the place was idiosyncratic and unrealistic. There was no way that a suburban community like this—especially with the new generation of hovering, overprotective parents—was going to sanction a former-landfill-turned-wilderness-fringe area where tires and broken baby dolls occasionally popped out of the ground. And unless you could justify its existence by turning it into an educational resource with guides and labels and classrooms, the people who wanted to turn it into ball fields or a golf course would carry the day.

So these people, ironically, were my best bet. Yet for all their good intentions, they were committed to destroying what I considered to be the essence of the place—its wildness. The only difference between their ideas and those of the sports boosters was that they would replace the wild with something naturalistic. At best, it would be an arboretum, and even that was probably unrealistic.

Once they finished dumping new soil all over and planting the "native species"—once it was put entirely under human control—other groups would see opportunities and would come forward with their own requests. Why not a playground (using natural materials, of course)? Picnic tables? A fragrance garden? A turtle pond? A carousel? Nobody could look into the plain face of nature anymore.

What had made these Meadowlands into this strange and wondrous wilderness had been the result of political accident, benign neglect, and the "Forbidden Forest" syndrome. It had been my good fortune to find nature, but my bad luck to find it growing on top of an inadequately covered landfill.

The low point of the meeting for me was when someone asked about the possibility of "a dog run."

Hawkins spread his arms wide in a gesture of great openness and tolerance. "We hadn't planned on it," he said. "But, well, *maybe.*"

My heart sank. A dog run? Maybe? This whole place was my dog run.

CHAPTER TWENTY-NINE

Below Freezing

The beginning of the end was a bad haircut. As fall had progressed into winter, Pete and Luke had gotten shaggier and shaggier. They both had a bad case of swamp odor. It was almost impossible to eat when the two of them were under the kitchen table.

We'd put off taking Pete to the groomer because they'd complained last time that he had become too difficult to work with. They suggested that we have him groomed at home. When I finally called for an appointment anyway, it was the beginning of the holiday season and they were booked through Christmas. It was the first week in January by the time we got them in. We gave the usual instructions for no-frills clips. And we specified that it not be too short, because it was winter.

But the dogs' coats must have crossed that threshold of shagginess, beyond which, the groomers say, they can't do anything but shear them. Because that's what they looked like when we went to pick them up—sheared down to the velvet undercoat. They felt like newborn lambs. The only exception was their faces, which had been given the boxy terrier look. Pete had bushy terrier brows and a squared-off muzzle so that he looked like a giant Scottie.

Then the thermometer's red line dropped to zero. The weather people reported ridiculous wind-chill temperatures like "28 below."

The prednisone tablets the vet had given Pete to reduce the arthritis inflammation and to give him more energy, animated him, but in a peculiar jerky way. And it gave him a freakish appetite. He was always hungry. And thirsty. He lapped up water by the quart and peed it out on the floor. Something—either old age or the steroids—was making his hair fall out. Friction points around his collar or the parts that rubbed against the floor when he lay down gave up their hair readily. He looked like he had mange.

Janet dug around in a bag of old camping clothes and found two insulated sweater-shirts for him. They were red with long sleeves. With some modifications he could wear one on the front and one on the back. It looked like a bright red leotard.

For outdoors, I added a sweater to the outfit.

The arctic weather froze the creek to a dull gray block from shore to shore. On nights like that, I often couldn't get Pete down the stairs—even just to the front lawn. Sometimes I carried him down to the car, though on the really cold nights, he never left it. Luke and I would do the walk without him.

The ground was frozen so hard around the ball fields that my feet barely registered the change from blacktop to frozen ground. I recalled reading in the newspaper that there were places in Antarctica, so-called "dry valleys," where conditions were not unlike those found in the plains of Mars. I could believe it. A drop of only thirty or forty degrees made everything seem alien. The whole natural world seemed locked away. No earthy smells or blossom fragrances, no chirping crickets, no peeping tree frogs, no birds settling down for the night. For the sake of some life, I would have welcomed the drone of a mosquito in my ear.

The air was so cold and dry that individual particles of snow blew around the parking lot like grains of sand. The wind would gather up a batch and send them scurrying across the asphalt until they vanished under a parking-lot log like smoke going under a door.

I read a long article in the *New Yorker* about the cycle of ice ages and interglacial periods. For the past million years or so, it seemed, warm periods had alternated with ice ages. This happened according to a fairly regular schedule: 10,000 years or so of warmth, followed by 90,000 years or so of cold. All of human civilization—this seemingly permanent accomplishment of ours—was merely a phenomenon of this in-between time. And we had used up 12,000 years of it already.

Later that winter came more of this cheerful scientific news. The *New York Times* reported that astrophysicists now believed, with some certainty, that the universe would expand forever, everything getting farther and farther apart. Energy would dissipate until there was nothing but coldness and darkness and stillness everywhere.

So that was the news from the big world: an ice age in the short term, an infinite void in the long term. On the home front, the living room, where Pete now slept on his dog bed, was getting a little drafty. Before I went to bed, I would cover him up and put a small heater on. He would open an eye and watch me without moving his head.

Below Freezing

Seeing him like that reminded me of the time Alex and I had taken him on a Cub Scout camping trip. Alex must have been about nine. Pete was maybe five. I was the miscast leader and had reserved one of the much sought after campsites at Sandy Hook. October, we fathers figured, would still be warm enough for camping because of the warmth retained by the ocean. But the last weekend of October straddled the beginning of November and when night came on, it got cold. And windy. We were in a clearing in a scrub forest and getting sandblasted. As we prepared to climb into our tent, Petey, thinking he might be excluded, gave us his best miserable, hangdog expression.

It wasn't necessary. I had even brought an old sleeping bag for him. So we all got in the tent, and I did my best to get Petey into or at least under his sleeping bag, though he continued to give me his worried look. Camping was usually something he loved, but the sides of the tent were flapping hard in the wind, and Pete wasn't happy with our situation. He seemed to miss the human life, whereas I was enjoying what I imagined was the canine life, our bodies pressed together like those of dogs in a den.

Now, here he was, almost ten years later, lying on his side on the fireplace hearth, his upside-eye watching.

It was beginning to feel like the end, and sometimes Pete seemed to be saying as much.

Finally, it was decided. It had to be done.

On the morning of the appointment at the vet's, Petey was up on his pins walking around. The night before, I couldn't get him into a standing position. Now, made abnormally hungry by the residual effect of the steroids, he was scavenging for cat food in the kitchen and looking to us for treats.

I sat at the kitchen table, miserable at this show of vigor. Of course, he had already pooped and peed on the floor. But seeing him like this, demanding food with short, wheezy barks, made it hard to justify what we were about to do.

The job fell to Alex and me. Claire and Janet would wait at home. Father and son got Pete in the car and drove mostly in silence. At the vet's office everyone wore a somber expression. After a while, we took Pete into an examination room. I kept petting his head, scratching his ears.

"He seems to know," said Alex.

I had the same feeling. How? I guess, the only way he could— through us. He had always been able to read our emotions. He did it through smell, voice, and body language. However he did it, he looked into us and perceived all our anxiety, fear, guilt, and sorrow. In response, he peed on the floor.

The vet had known Pete for all these fifteen years. He was the one who first explained to me when I was puzzled by this new breed of dog's relatively sweet demeanor (I had been used to terriers) that poodles are "lovers."

The vet seemed genuinely sad. I signed the forms. He said he would give Pete an overdose of an anesthesia, so that he would simply go to sleep. He assured me it would be painless. As to the remains, he offered us three choices—mass cremation, individual cremation, and burial. I asked about the prices, and though individual cremation was twice the group cremation price, I said yes to that. It was foolish, I supposed. Who would know what they really did with your dog's body? Years ago, our paper ran an expose on a pet cemetery operation where the animals that were supposedly buried and cremated had simply been thrown in big trenches.

I said I didn't want to be there when they gave him the injection.

Alex and I had discussed this in the waiting room, and he had said he felt the same way. But, there, in the exam room, he suddenly changed his mind and said that he would stay with Pete, so that, he said, "he has someone he knows there with him."

I went out into the waiting room. After a few minutes, a boy came in with a turtle in a plastic box. He slouched down on the seat next to me. Then his father, who had been parking the car, came in. Looking at this boy with his pet, I kept thinking of a picture of Alex and Pete that was on our mantel. Alex was about four when the picture was taken. It was July and he had just returned from day camp at one of the town parks. He had come home dirty and happy, his still-pudgy legs smudged with mud. And he had one arm slung around Pete—still a big puppy—in the easy, familiar way that a young boy pals around with a dog.

But Pete could play the surrogate parent, too. When the kids were young and I had child-launching responsibilities, he was like the family butler, annoyingly punctual, running from room to room nudging the children awake, checking on my progress.

God forbid that I had to double back for a forgotten lunchbox. For then he would give me one of his disapproving looks. If there was more than one delay, he'd give me that supercilious snort, which would remind me that—despite his untrimmed appearance—he was a *French* poodle after all.

Now it had come to this. Three of us had positioned ourselves at some tolerable distance from what was happening. Janet and Claire had said goodbye to Petey back at the house. I had come this far, but didn't want to be on the other side of that door. And there was Alex. It wasn't a natural role for him. At age six or seven, when he was practically mesmerized by any movie, he had to leave the room when the family watched *The Bear*, a French film about an orphaned grizzly cub. He could watch incredibly violent movies like *RoboCop*, where people were riddled with machine gun fire, but not a scene in which a mother bear appeared to be shot by hunters.

Where had all this time gone? Sometimes, when something like this happens, I think you mourn not just over the loss of a pet, but for that simple and terrible thing: the passage of time. It was too easy to look back. When you lived it, it was like traversing the Grand Canyon on foot. But having reached the other side, you could just turn back and look across the whole gulf. All that living, compressed into a glance.

They were taking a long time in there. I looked toward the glass-windowed door where I knew Alex would appear. I wondered if he would come carrying the red T-shirts. My eyes drifted up to the clippings on the office bulletin board. There was one from my own paper with one of our corny headlines: DOG GONE TECHNOLOGY.

And now I wished that in the last year I had just gotten cozy with Pete more, stroked him a little more. Old dogs get brittle, stiff beneath your caressing hand, but it's not their fault. And I began to berate myself for making him go out on those walks.

I had told myself that it was some important purchase on life for him. The walk! To walk was to be alive! To lie down was to die! *C'mon Pete. We need to go out.* But I was beginning to think that I hadn't been doing it so much for him as for myself.

It was me. I had become the one who needed to go on walks. We had reversed roles.

I further realized that on some childish level, I had been angry with him for not wanting to go anymore. I wanted Pete to drag himself up with his last bit of strength like some enfeebled sled dog in a Jack London story standing ready for the harness. I wanted it to still be this important thing for him. But it wasn't. And the worst thought was that maybe he exaggerated his helplessness sometimes in order to get out of it, not realizing—because it was beyond his imagining—that these sorts of things were being put on a scale in this . . . *case* that was being made. *We can barely lift him. Couldn't get him out of the car . . . He sees how hopeless it is . . . Maybe it's time . . .*

The steroids had been a mistake. They just made him crazier. We should have just made him comfortable . . . We . . .

Finally Alex appeared. His cheeks were red and glazed with tears. He turned away from me as he came into the room, as if to hide it.

Outside I told him that he'd been very brave, that I was proud of him. We got in the car, and after we'd driven a few blocks he started talking about it: "It happened so fast. They had trouble finding the vein at first. Then they did, and a second or so after the injection, he just slumped. I could feel the life go out of him."

I pictured them listening for his heartbeat with a stethoscope. The road looked blurry in front of me.

At home, Janet and Claire didn't come to the door. They stayed back in the kitchen, as if to delay the news. On the way through the dining room, I saw that Janet had put a picture of Pete on the piano—the one of him jumping off a rock into the lake in the Adirondacks. It had always been a happy picture in our album, but now the leap looked metaphorical and tragic.

Alex and I walked into the kitchen. Now it was official. The bells could toll. In most grieving situations, some people stay strong and offer comfort to the others. But who in this room could stand outside this grief? What a picture we made. All four of us, leaning on each other, tears streaming down our faces.

Three nights later, I was out with Luke. We were walking on the edge of the riding center grounds. It was late, very late. It was the time of night that Scandinavian legends called the "Hour of the Wolf," the hour when demons, ghosts, and nasty spirits haunted and harassed the sleepless.

It was god-awful dark. There wasn't even a moon to nail your hopes on. A moon can be a companion on a dark night, a fellow traveler. It can dome the sky, lift it like a tent pole. Even a star or two can prick the blackness and make some breathing room. But this night was as close and low-ceilinged as a subway tunnel.

The cold spell had broken. The snow beneath my feet was melting. I was up to my ankles in a miniature fog. I felt like

Gulliver in the land of the Lilliputians. On an impulse, I walked toward the stables. What harm? No one was around. The world was asleep and in this kind of darkness, Luke and I were almost equally invisible.

Luke quickly got out ahead, establishing his place in front. But I was no longer in the middle, no longer framed by two dogs. I missed that feeling of having Pete back there. I realized now how much he'd been like my sea anchor. Now I was uncomfortably light—off-kilter, listing now to port and now to starboard, my bow dipping too low in the waves.

I had been surprised at the outpouring of sympathy from the community. People we hadn't heard from in years called the house. Some sent cards. Boys from our baseball team, who remembered Pete as the mascot, called and wanted to get together with Alex to reminisce.

I kept tormenting myself with certain details: the way Pete arranged himself so trustingly in the back of the station wagon. The way he sat at my feet in the waiting room and peed. And the way I guided him, his lumpy, gimpy rear end down the hall to his death.

I found myself thinking back to that period when Janet and I separated and I lived in a small apartment on the other side of town. I still came back every morning to get the kids ready for school. By arriving before they were awake, I felt like I was getting away with something, preserving the illusion that I had been there all night. Why, here was Dad, just as always, making breakfast and finding backpacks.

To whatever degree the children bought into the illusions of normalcy, Pete was not fooled. He received my arrival with neither the bark of alarm that he used with strangers nor the heralding bark that he used with family members. He greeted me in silence, with a tentative, ambivalent tail wag. He knew nothing of separation or visitation. He understood things on a primitive level. He wanted me to understand that this would not do, and that I couldn't expect to spend so much time away from the den and still retain my position in the pack. His instincts had a template for me: the lone wolf, the male who had been driven out or left the pack for some reason and now lived a solitary existence.

Things were better between us on the walk. Out in the woods or the Meadowlands we could be as we were. Sometimes, afterward, I brought Pete to my apartment. I imagined that he would prefer to be with me than alone in the house, but it was for my benefit as well. The first time, I watched from my desk as he sniffed around and tried to make sense of his master's presence in this new den. He'd given the place a thorough once-over and then settled to the floor with a sigh. I wanted him to put his canine blessing on this new arrangement. But he never understood, never approved, never seemed comfortable in this alternate universe I had created.

People called it magical thinking if you imagined the dead were still around. To my mind, it was the opposite. It required magical thinking to believe that someone—human or animal—could be with us, then not, their bodies suddenly an empty shell.

As we approached the stables—a huge, barnlike building and several smaller, low-slung ones—I picked up the smells—the manure, the hay, the horses. Without the young women in their fancy riding gear, the place looked more plain, like a ranch or a farm. I could be up in Vermont. It was like a dream. Clamped onto the back of the barn was a huge funnel-shaped dispenser that must have contained feed or oats or whatever it was that horses ate. There was the huge shed for indoor riding and several narrow buildings that must have contained the stables. A car was parked next to one of those buildings. Someone, I realized, had to be here at all hours in case of fire or some other emergency. I wondered if that someone was awake, whether he made night patrols.

But all the buildings were dark. All around us, I imagined sleeping horses. Luke must smell them, I thought. And there would be the scents of other creatures, the ones that were always around barns—the mice, the cats, those border collies I sometimes saw. Where were they?

In the dim light, I saw the face of a horse in a window. It was looking out at us. The window was just a regular sash window, the same style and size as one in a human house. But in this building it was positioned at one end of a stall, so that this horse had a view. I had read somewhere that horses didn't sleep very much—only a few hours a night. They were natural insomniacs.

It momentarily cheered me, seeing this horse looking at me like this, this fellow creature, so silent and calm. I leaned in for a closer look. The horse's long face had what seemed like a human expression, with large, long-lashed eyes. Above each eye was a curving brow, a nest of arching wrinkles like those that gave human eyes an attitude of sympathy. Its lower lip rolled out slightly and the sensitive, downward curves at the corners made the face look wise and judicious. It didn't seem just human. It seemed more than human—like Jonathan Swift's superior equine race.

There was something so strange about the setup: the horse on the inside of the window, me on the outside. Luke was off sniffing at the base of the barn wall, so the horse and I were, so to speak, alone. Between us were layers of glass and screening, like the barrier between the priest and the penitent in a church confessional—or that between a visitor and an inmate in a jail. The horse's compassionate demeanor seemed to offer forgiveness. At the same time, its circumstances—behind this human window, mutely gazing out, a prisoner, really—felt like a silent rebuke to our assumed dominion over animals. Who were we to decide, based on mere cleverness, when other creatures should live and die? Who was I to rule in these matters?

Luke and I walked back to the car. It was still dark, but some of the cloud cover had lifted and stars glimmered in the openings.

A few years ago, I had had an idea for a book. The premise was that I could find meaning in an ordinary dog walk. Because I was an art critic, there seemed a special irony in this. On the interest scale—the continuum from boring to exciting—art was considered the polar opposite of dog walking. A work of art, after all, was supposed to be loaded with significance and meaning, as carefully packed as a fireworks missile. Even bad art was supposed to be more interesting than a walk around the block tethered to a domesticated member of the canine family, an activity whose primary purpose was for the animal to handle its excretory needs.

Sure enough, the world opened up to me in unexpected ways. And I thought I had made some discovery: that this tiny little area of life could be a wedge into the whole amorphous experience of living. A task with no meaning? No problem! Boredom? Not to worry! There was nothing that couldn't be coaxed out of it.

I thought I was carrying out some sort of Thoreau-like experiment in living. Or had found what was sought by the "contemplative man," as Walton subtitled *The Compleat Angler*. But losing Pete—and knowing that I had played a role in his death—had left me reeling. I had gone astray, and now I wasn't sure where I was, or whether, in all my excitement over these discoveries, I had missed the whole point of everything—which had less to do with the weird wonders of the Meadowlands—and more to do with Pete in the life of our family. Somehow I had lost my way on a simple dog walk.

CHAPTER THIRTY

Lost and Found

You find your way. You lose your way. You find your way again.

Without Pete, Luke couldn't stay in the car by himself. I'd go into a store for a minute and he'd have a panic attack. I'd come back to find claw marks and small tears in the upholstery. I realized that in all his life he had never been alone. He had gone straight from the litter to the company of Pete.

Now both of us were lost. Out in the dark ball field, I'd see what I thought were the silhouettes of two dogs, but it was just Luke—running here and there so fast that he seemed to be in two places at once.

As for finding any larger meaning in the walks, well, forget it. I couldn't remember what that had been about. I was back to square one. For the first time in years, I began to look at other dog walkers as if they might show me the way. What were *they* doing? What were *they* thinking?

Of course, what many were doing was . . . something else. Dog walking, which required only one hand at most, had become a perfect cell-phone-talking opportunity. That classic suburban tableau of the man standing impatiently while his dog lazily anointed the base of a tree had been replaced by a tableau of a dog tugging impatiently while the man lingered, talking on his phone.

One day, deep in the Meadowlands reeds and feeling lost to the world, I heard a voice. Taking a few more steps forward on what was a very narrow and tentative trail, I saw the head of a man I recognized. He had stopped ahead of me. I couldn't see his dog, a black-and-white pit bull, though I knew it had to be somewhere around his feet. He was the only other dog walker I knew who regularly tramped through this thick growth. We sometimes passed each other, but we only exchanged slight nods and a mumbled "Hey." I'd judged him a solitary, slightly misanthropic, *Deer Hunter* kind of guy who needed to be alone with nature. Now, here he was, up to his ears in reeds and gabbing like a teenager outside the convenience store. I got close enough to see the black wires dangling down from his ears. He was so distracted that he never even noticed us, and the dog, who I'm sure knew our scent, saw no point in alerting him.

Another group combined dog walking with some sport or exercise. They jogged down the street attached to their dogs with stretchy cords. Or put backpacks on their dogs and took them hiking. I read about a sport called skijoring, in which dogs pulled people on cross-country skis. Once I saw a young mother doing four things at once: jogging, pushing a baby stroller, dog walking, and listening to an iPod.

One day in the park, I watched somewhat enviously as a man threw a Frisbee to his yellow Lab. They put on a terrific performance, these two. The man made gorgeous straight throws so that the disk seemed to hover and the dog arrived just in time to snatch it from the air. They repeated the trick without a slip. Luke watched with keen interest, feeling the tug of his retriever genes, perhaps, and I, watching the Lab prance back with the Frisbee, tail and head held high, found myself feeling bad that I had never taken the time to teach my dogs how to do any tricks.

Unable to shake this hollow feeling and sensing that Luke deserved some canine companionship, I decided to try the dog park.

Luke was a sociable dog. He was fine in one-on-one meetings with dogs in the park or the Meadowlands, so there was reason to be optimistic, but the dog park presented him with a social situation that he seemed to find disturbing. To the human members, perhaps, the situation seemed as natural as bringing a child to a playground. *Run off and play now!* But dogs aren't children. They are pack animals, so naturally, they formed a pack. Given the constant comings and goings, however, it was a very chaotic pack. With every opening and closing of the gate, with every dog added or subtracted, the dynamics changed. Hierarchies had to be reordered. The situation made it impossible for any dog to know where it stood for more than a few moments.

This situation, with its ever-shifting alliances and animosities, made my male dog anxious. The pack ran from one end of the area to the other, its members barking, nipping, and jostling one another. Some dogs were clearly having the time of their lives. Others sought respite on the sidelines. Luke watched from under one of the picnic tables, lightly panting.

Human conflicts mirrored those of the dogs. People with timid or easygoing dogs resented those who had aggressive dogs. Some dogs ate other dog's poop. Some dogs were droolers and covered others with saliva. Some were humpers.

Perhaps Luke would have worked out his place in that ever-shifting pack had we stayed. Perhaps I, too, would have gotten used to it and forgotten why I ever enjoyed traipsing around in the Meadowlands. But I didn't think so.

I had had enough. What I wanted in the morning was a feeling of going forth, of striding out into life.

Still in a slump a week or so later, and casting about for dog-walking inspiration, I decided one day to take Luke to Central Park. Why not? For years, I'd been meaning to do something like this. I loved the park. I had sketched there, been to concerts and Shakespeare plays there, and even written articles about its design—but I had never walked a dog there. I drove to upper Fifth Avenue late on a weekday afternoon, planning my arrival to coincide with the time when parking along some streets turned legal. I found an empty spot north of 90th Street, which, according to the sign, permitted parking at the stroke of 6:00, about ten minutes from then. So I had a short wait.

The late-afternoon sun reflected off the buildings. Inside the park, I could see people walking on paths at different levels. I thought of Olmsted's three-dimensional landscape paintings. His special effects were still working. This scene looked like one of American Postimpressionist Maurice Prendergast's colorful patchwork tableaus. A young man in loose-fitting clothes came by walking five dogs. A professional dog walker. How, I had often wondered, did they do it? I'd seen them with up to ten dogs—the leashes splayed out in their hands like the strings on a bunch of balloons. They never seemed stressed or trying too hard. What was their secret?

I watched these five dogs. They walked next to the young man, keeping step with his stride. They pulled none of the usual leashed-dog shenanigans. They didn't try to pull, or stop to sniff, or race ahead. Nope, they just walked calmly along, either a little in front or a little behind. Did these dogs undergo some lengthy training before they could enter the program? Were they drugged? Or was the trick in very careful screening? *Only mature, preferably aged and highly cooperative dogs need apply.*

A small Jeep pulled into the space ahead of us. A guy with a ponytail got out, opened the back, and released a yellow shepherd-type dog. I watched the two of them walk into the park. I looked at my watch. It was exactly six o'clock. There is no clever thing you can come up with in New York City—*Hey, I'll drive to Central Park, arrive just before six so I can park, and walk my dog in the park*—that someone hasn't thought of already.

I leashed Luke and we entered the park at 90th Street. Beyond the gate, there was a small plaza and beyond that a stairway leading up to the reservoir. The track around this raised bowl was one of the city's most popular running locations. Runners went up the stairs dry and composed and came down flushed and perspiring. The tired ones headed for the plaza's drinking fountain, which, I was pleased to see, had two bowls, an upper one for humans and a lower one for dogs. I took Luke over and pressed the pedal with my foot to give him a drink.

Walkers came and went with dogs of every imaginable breed and size: Labradors, goldens, poodles, sheep dogs, Welsh corgis, terriers, dachshunds, borzois, setters, Afghans, bulldogs. I liked being among all these devoted dog walkers. I knew they were devoted, because to keep a dog in the city, you had to be. You had to keep up your side of the dog-walking bargain. You couldn't backslide, like the suburban dog walker, by putting the dog out in a yard. Just getting a dog out of an apartment building could be an ordeal. It meant encountering other dogs, small children, fragile old ladies and dog phobics in narrow hallways, tiny elevators, and public lobbies. It meant training your dog not to regard these intermediate places as suitable for elimination just because he was outside the walls of his apartment.

You might expect people in these situations to have smaller dogs than people living elsewhere, but they didn't. Their dogs were just as big as the ones I saw around my town. And, this being Manhattan, both dogs and their owners displayed more style and sophistication than their suburban counterparts. I saw a man walking his Jack Russell terrier on top of a four-foot-high wall while he, holding the leash, walked on the adjacent path.

We reached the pump house at the south end of the reservoir, crossed a handsome little bridge, and arrived behind the Metropolitan Museum of Art. All the magnolias were in bloom, their pink and white blossoms opening like parrots' beaks. Daffodils waved their perky heads on the slopes.

Nearby was *Cleopatra's Needle,* a red granite obelisk given to the city by the Egyptian government in 1881. The name is misleading, since the obelisk was made many centuries before Cleopatra's time. Its 3,300-year-old hieroglyphs celebrate Ramesses II, the same pharaoh of Percy Shelley's famous poem, whose broken, half-buried statue pathetically declares: "My name is Ozymandias, king of kings/ Look on my works, ye Mighty, and despair!"

We passed the broad Sheep Meadow, which was fenced off for grass growing. People zipped by us on roller skates and bicycles. Others were jogging or walking their dogs. Everyone was doing something.

I decided to visit Cedar Hill, the Bunker Hill of the leash-law revolution. Here, in the mid 1990s, dog walkers made their first heroic stand, getting front-page coverage in the *New York Times* over their fight to let their dogs run free. They eventually won a concession from the city: dogs could be unleashed early in the morning or late at night, but not between 9:00 a.m. and 9:00 p.m. The issue remains volatile and the compromise is constantly under attack, review, and reconsideration by people on both sides.

This evening, perhaps because it was still too early, there was only one dog walker there, a woman throwing a stick for her sheep dog. I let Luke loose for a few minutes to play. It looked like a good dog-romping area. The steep little hill, I could see, helped to keep dogs in sight, with gravity slowing any frisky runners and the cedar trees at the top defining the boundary.

After his romp, Luke and I walked up to the top of the hill, where I found a rustic Adirondack-style bench to sit on. We were just high enough to see out to Fifth Avenue, where lights were beginning to wink on in the apartments. I looked in the other direction, into the depths of the park and remembered how, coming here with a sketchpad, Olmsted's pastoral illusions had once been plenty of nature for me.

Luke made a barely audible woof. He was looking at something behind me. I turned and saw, in among the trees of Olmsted's Cedar Hill, a homeless man. He was lying in a sleeping bag, up on one elbow, smoking a cigarette.

It was funny, when you thought about it. Here, in this artfully composed landscape, the one unplanned thing, the one wild element was . . . a human being.

As we traced our steps back to the car, the park's old-style street lamps were coming on. The Metropolitan Museum of Art loomed on our right. Statues in brightly lit galleries stared out at us. I recognized Auguste Rodin's medieval martyrs, the *Burghers of Calais.* These craggy figures were bound together by ropes and chains, heavy with doom. Nearby were their opposites, light, sleek Aristide Maillol torsos, sexy and full of vitality.

Everyone was heading for the exits. Bicyclists swooped up behind us with calls of "On your left," or "On your right." Ahead was a slower-moving conveyance commandeered by a stout bag lady. Dozens of stuffed shopping bags festooned her cluster of carts. Tied to the front—as if helping to pull the load, but not really doing so—was a dog. I studied the dog. It was ordinary and of medium size. What made it different from all the other dogs out in the park was that it was not out for a recreational walk. This was its way of life. My first impulse was to pity it, yet, it didn't look unhappy or poorly cared for. On further reflection, I realized that it had something other dogs didn't: a fully shared life with its human companion. It never spent a day alone in an apartment waiting for its person to come home.

Out on Fifth Avenue, the Guggenheim Museum's spiral rotunda glowed like a flying saucer. Instead of going straight back to the car, we detoured over to Madison Avenue. I'd walked these streets many times, but doing it with a dog felt different. Having a dog, I realized, tagged me as a resident of the neighborhood, and so Luke and I slipped into new identities. As we strolled past the boutiques and specialty food shops of Carnegie Hill, I constructed our new life. We came to a French bakery and I tied Luke to a parking meter and ducked inside for a baguette. Now, with the long bread tucked under my arm my impersonation seemed complete: French bread and French poodle—even if the poodle was a bit shaggy. I ripped off a chunk of the crusty bread, gave it to Luke, ripped off another for myself, and fleshed out my life, one based, I decided, on inherited wealth. I pictured my furnishings and my new wardrobe, taking cues from the antiques stores and men's shops we passed.

Soon we were back at the car. I gave us each more bread, made a few notes in my pocket notebook, and started the engine. Luke settled into the wagon's capacious back and positioned himself in the center, where he could monitor activities on all four sides of the car.

For the first time since Petey died, I had felt completely alive on a walk.

CHAPTER THIRTY-ONE

Horse Way

One sunny September day, Luke and I found ourselves in horse country. Picture this scene if you will: a white rail fence along a great steeplechase ring—an enclosure the size of a football field with an earthen ramp at one end. Beyond are more corrals—ovals and rectangles of different sizes. Luke, twenty feet ahead, detours impatiently into the side brush to do his business. He looks anxiously over his shoulder at me, concerned that I might get to the corner of the corral and go around the bend before him. This, his expression tells me, is too important a transition to entrust to a mere human.

The turn takes us into a grassy, sun-dappled corridor, woods on one side, a line of corrals on the other, and at the end, the creek.

Our friends, the horses, are already waiting for us.

About a dozen equine heads have turned in our direction. The ones in the more distant corrals simply watch, heads poking up above the maze of fences, ears erect, profiles as distinct as chess pieces. But the nearer ones amble over—*ka-klump, ka-klump, ka-klump*. They hang their long faces over the rail.

Oh, those horse faces! I've looked at countless paintings of horses, all of them focused on the power and grace of their bodies. No other animal has inspired so many admiring images. The art of the museums, however, doesn't prepare you for the close-up sweetness of equine faces. I can see why young girls fall in love with horses. The illustrators who do the covers for books such as *National Velvet* and *My Friend Flicka* exaggerate horses' anthropomorphic charm much less than you would think. It is as much the opposite, that the museum-quality artists steer away from such character-izations for fear of being snared in sentimentality. After all, what is a serious artist going to do with that adorable forelock that spills forward between the horse's peaked ears? And those large liquid eyes with the long lashes? And the mouth with the mobile lips that extend animatedly when they nibble or—as with that horse I saw at the window that night—display in the downturned corners an expression that can only be described as judicious.

A frisky brown stallion drops his enormous bulk to the ground, flips onto his back and kicks his hooves in the air, scratching his back like a dog. For such large ruminants, they are surprisingly play-ful. I pat their hard foreheads, run my hand along their smooth, muscled necks, and feed them handfuls of grass. Equine attention has something a little uncanny about it. Compared to say, cows, or even dogs, horses seem so face-to-face personable and engaging, eager, it would seem, for some real conversation.

Next time, I'll bring apples, I think. A tall black mare with a blaze dips her head down to give Luke a sniff. For Luke, the huge muzzle with the twitching nostrils is too much friendliness, and he scampers backwards. Then, embarrassed at his timidity, he barks at the retreating horse and charges back to the fence in a face-saving effort that fools neither the horse nor me.

As to how we got into horse country, it started with shake-ups at the local riding stables. Someone finally caught on that an exclusive club for the international horsey set was being run on county parkland. After a few weeks of juicy news stories about Beverly Hills doctors, world-class show jumpers, million-dollar horses, and lucrative subletting deals, topped by the revelation that the manager was hundreds of thousands of dollars behind in his rent, the parks department took the facility back on behalf of the people (who, up until then, were having a hard time booking a lesson). After the scalawag was evicted and the fancy horses and their owners sent packing, the county bought its own stable of horses and promised to make lessons affordable to all.

Right away the once-forbidding aristocratic enclave seemed approachable. I no longer worried that, as trespassers, we were going to be attacked by Dobermans or run off the property by rich girls in Land Rovers.

Then, something even better happened. Heavy-duty brush cutters and mowers were brought in to clear the dense thicket of shrubs and reeds behind the corrals. They pushed this tangle back a good fifteen feet, creating a nice, wide corridor that became our new gateway into the wild.

We had been through a lot of landscape in the Meadowlands. We had pushed through jungly wildness, had been chased by sudden squalls, had seen the Overpeck flood its banks—in short, had had all those jaw-dropping experiences of unrestrained nature that the transcendentalists called a pipeline to God. Now there was a prelude to all that, a scene that embodied the pastoral beauty that

Horse Way

Olmsted sought to evoke, but without any contrivance. This was the real thing, the kind of scenery that inspired the pictures that inspired Olmsted in the first place.

After we got to the end of the horse reception line, Luke and I would find ourselves on the high bank of the creek, a crossroads with a different view in each direction. To our right, the stables and barn with its steaming haystack and smell of manure; straight ahead, the sparkling creek and the inlets and sand spits of its far bank; and to our left, the path along the creek with its whispering cottonwoods.

We always took the creek path, but without knowing for sure how far we'd get. The brush cutters had cleared a little ways in. Beyond, it was the usual Meadowlands experience of following a trail that progressively narrowed until it finally stopped altogether. Lately, however, I'd noticed places where the narrow trail continued without petering out, as if a very thin person had been tramping through.

One day I saw a little heap of shiny oblong pellets. I recognized them from a picture in one of my field guides as deer droppings. This was the first time I'd seen signs of deer in the Meadowlands. It didn't entirely surprise me, given the reports lately of deer coming down along the Palisades. People in towns just north of us were seeing deer in their backyards.

Soon came a third confirmation, a crisply defined cloven print in soft mud.

North had been off the dog-walking circuit for several months, distracted by medical problems, family responsibilities, his job—all the things that can collectively convince you that you have no time for something as trivial as dog walking—unless, of course, you are the one with the dog.

Spring pulled him out of his burrow. I took him to horse country, and he surprised me by knowing all about these animals. He'd learned to ride during summers spent at his uncle's farm in rural New Jersey. Always the scholar, he was soon schooling me on the proper horse nomenclature. A horse was never brown, he said, but "chestnut." Tan ones were "palominos." Others were "piebald," "dapple gray," and "pinto."

After that I took him along the creek trail, and we saw the deer droppings and the heart-shaped hoof marks. I'd been studying my field guide to tracking and was looking forward to the day when I could scan an area and say something like, *"Looks like two does were browsing here. Then a third came along, a mature buck. It's rutting season, so he was probably following their scent. Over here, you can see how they all galloped off . . ."*

"What can you tell from these?" North asked me in front of just such a cluster of tracks. I bent over to look, admiring the beauty of the marks, the way the soft mud had come up between the cleft in the hooves, how the tips were so elegantly pointed, like expensive women's shoes. I looked for the two little dew-claw marks behind the prints, which, I'd learned, could be used to distinguish between front feet and back feet. I looked for signs of overlapping tracks or evidence of rear hooves marking in front of front hooves to tell what gait they had been using. Finally, I stood up, rubbing my chin.

"Well?" asked North.

"Well, I'm pretty sure there were some deer here," I said.

"Brilliant," said North.

"Tracking is tricky," I said. "Subtle. I haven't mastered it yet."

"Uh-huh," said North.

"Anyway," I said, "I'll show you something better." I led North off the main trail, following the skinniest of paths through a place where a web of thin vines had pulled down the phragmites. This had been going on for several seasons, this battle between the invasive phragmites and the now even more invasive "mile-a-minute vine." In the eyes of the native-species crowd, this was like a fight between two monsters, Godzilla versus Mothra. The vines died off at the end of the season, leaving a dense tangle, like a reddish netting, on top of the half-fallen-but-not-yet-vanquished reeds. The result, after the weight of winter snows, was a strange, undulating landscape that looked like a place "wrapped" by the contemporary artist Christo.

"Aren't there ticks in here?" asked North.

"Haven't been any yet," I said. "We'll check ourselves back at the car."

North grunted, not entirely trusting me on this matter of the ticks.

"Look," I said, pointing down to these smooth depressions in a low place in the vine-and-reed bed. "This is where they sleep. You can see the imprint left by their bodies."

"Huh," said North, looking around. "It's perfectly concealed. You could walk right by and not know they were in here."

He had put his finger on what I loved about having the deer around. A Meadowlands that contained such large and beautiful animals could, at any moment, become a simulacrum of the African Savanna. Ten minutes later Luke made that happen, flushing out a trio of deer that bounded off like leaping gazelles, white tails flipped up like flags. North and I stared in wonder. North, for once, had no literary quote for the occasion.

Luke came trotting back, his tongue dangling out of his mouth.

It was one of those days where you just felt like walking and walking. North seemed up for anything. Soon, the ShopRite supermarket came into sight. Around the bend was our old park, still closed after almost two years of work. It was practically a year behind schedule.

"Want to see our old stomping grounds?" I asked.

"Whatever's on the tour," said North.

The weeping willow tree that used to dangle its branches like a beaded curtain had been removed, so that the park came into view sooner than it used to. Work was winding down, plus it was a weekend, so the big earthmoving machines stood idle.

The last time I was here, the place looked like it had been bombed. Huge craters and heaps of dirt stood everywhere. Long trenches had been dug for drainage pipes. I couldn't figure out what they were doing. Now I saw. All this had been prelude, apparently, to making the land *flat*. The meadow was to be some sort of athletic field. Every crease and roll had been ironed out of it.

"This was our meadow," I said, gesturing to the area immediately in front of us.

North looked dumbstruck.

"Remember those golfers? They used to practice little chip shots there. They would drop out of sight down in those dips, remember?" I felt like I was talking about some remote period of our childhoods. The rest of the park was even less recognizable. It wasn't just that there were new structures. Nothing was the same color or texture. A once-soft greenish-brown landscape now looked metallic and plastic. In place of the dusty baseball diamonds and cinder running track were stadium bleachers and synthetic grass carpets. Instead of trees, there were light stanchions and scoreboards.

"What's all this for?" North finally said.

"I think they're calling it a *regional sports complex*," I said. "It's for high school and Little League."

"It looks like a pro's training camp," he said.

I reminded him of the political history: how the town to the north had rejected the county's plans for a second such facility, and the county, having already budgeted the money for two, simply funneled it all into one.

"That's why there are forty-foot light stanchions every ten feet," I said. "That's why the bleachers look big enough for a minor league stadium. Every few hundred feet they had to build *something*. They had a lot of money to spend."

"Why don't the politicians just *give* our money to the contractors, and leave us our parks," North said.

Luke had trotted over to the edge of the field where he used to do his business, but he was blocked by a black plastic construction barrier. On the other side was where we'd found the ladybugs. Had they survived the disruption?

Ladybug, Ladybug, fly away home . . .

We walked toward the creek. When we got to the place where we used to turn left to walk along the upper bank, there was now an asphalt walkway.

"Our grassy path," I said.

"Macadamized," North said.

And so we headed back for the wild.

About a month later, during a premature cold snap in October, North joined us again, as did a border collie from the riding center. This had happened a few times before. His name was Jester, according to his tag. He would first come across the corrals barking, then, when it became clear we weren't going to invade his territory, he'd drop the guard-dog pretense and come over to socialize. He and Luke would take off in a spirited game of tag or keep-away. After five or ten minutes of this, Jester would answer the call of duty and head back to the stables.

So there were four of us that day on the creekside trail. The sun was up, but the puddles were all frozen and the grass was clotted with frost. The dogs were picking up sticks and chasing each other, embroidering the straight stitch of our human walk.

North was relating some classroom incident involving a student and a cell phone, when I spotted a garter snake by the side of the road. We regularly saw snakes—they often sunned themselves in the middle of the path—but this snake was dead. Its body was frozen into an S-shape curve and displayed a deep red gash about a third of the way down its length. It looked as if it had died in the middle of a struggle. It was as stiff as a stick.

North and I both studied it.

"What do you think happened to it?" I asked North.

"Some sort of bite. . . . Maybe an owl or a hawk."

It wasn't unusual for us to find the remains of killed animals—a decapitated mouse, a heap of bird feathers, and a few clots of gore.

"*Et in Arcadia ego*," said North, which was his usual erudite response to such finds. It was Latin for "Even in Arcadia I exist," meaning there was no escape from death, even in paradise.

"Strange, though," I said. "That whatever killed it didn't eat it."

North shrugged.

"Garter snakes release an odor," I said. "Maybe an animal bit into it—then dropped it."

"The malodorous defense was too little, too late."

"Right," I said.

The snake, frozen in this stop-action pose, looked fake, like a sight gag. I tossed it into the reeds.

And so we continued along. A barrel-chested hawk glared down on us from the bleached branches of a dead tree.

"There's a suspect," North said. "Look at that cold, murderous eye."

On we walked. The dogs raced happily about, circling around us and running far ahead.

Soon we came upon another snake. It was dead, just like the first one, with the same kind of wound, in what looked to be the same place.

"This is weird," I said. "Something has killed this snake in the same way."

North studied Snake Number Two. "Maybe some organ burst in both of them," he said. "That would explain the similar location. A heart attack, or something."

"No," I said, sensing the presence of the Crackpot Naturalist. "This is a bite. I can see puncture marks there."

He studied it but said nothing.

I tossed the second snake into the brush.

The concept of "foul play" is not supposed to enter into the struggle for survival among animals. In their world, killing each other is the accepted norm. Still, sometimes, you can't help seeing a malevolent hand—or paw, or talon—at work.

"He kills for pleasure," North said. "What does that tell you?"

"That he'll do it again?"

"Precisely."

"A snake serial killer," I said.

North pondered this. "Actually," he said, "it should probably be a serial snake killer."

"Oh?"

"The way you said it makes it sound as if the snake *is* the serial killer."

"Uh-oh," I said. "Look!"

There on the ground was a third snake. Dead. Curled up the same way. With the same type of wound a third of the way down its body.

"Good God!" said North.

Before I could pick it up, Luke swooped in out of nowhere and snatched it off the ground. Then, frozen snake in his mouth, he went running down the trail, Jester in pursuit. As they ran into the sun, Luke made a comical profile, the stiff curvy snake sticking out of his mouth. Then he dropped it and the two of them ran off in search of some new amusement. It lay on the trail as we approached. Snake Number Four.

"It was always the same snake?" North muttered in disbelief.

It was true. Poodles, I reminded North, are retrievers. "They're always picking up whatever you drop or throw."

We walked in silence for a few moments, both of us trying to figure out how we had failed to observe the repeated fetchings of the same snake.

"That one time we were looking up at the hawk," said North.

"And busy theorizing," I said. "Isn't there a *Winnie the Pooh* story like this?"

North smiled. "Pooh and Piglet are tracking something in the snow. And they keep going around this tree . . ."

"And seeing more and more tracks . . ." It was coming back to me. "What was it that they thought they were tracking?"

"The Woozle," said North.

"The Woozle," I repeated. "Long live the Woozle."

CHAPTER THIRTY-TWO

Into the Night

Lately, Luke and I have been edging toward the nocturnal. We spend less time on the morning walk and stay out longer at night. I'm not sure why. For a while, work crews were in the Meadowlands drilling test wells, and the noise and destruction drove us away. That's how it started.

Then I came to like the dark. The night has always seemed bigger than the day—and wilder. Darkness reduces overly detailed things to sharp silhouettes—the rooflines of the distant barns and stables, the inkblot shapes of the trees, the tilting utility poles marching along the railroad tracks. Puddles shine bright as mirrors. Cirrostratus clouds the size of continents inch across the moonlit sky. I assemble it night after night like an old wooden puzzle. The pieces snap into place. *Click, click, click.* And there it is. Everything fits.

Deer, browsing in the greener front of the park, pick up our scent and gallop for the woods, passing so close I can feel the *thump* of their hooves through the soles of my shoes. Luke is off in ecstatic pursuit, and I watch how differently the two animals run: Luke, low, parallel to the ground, his body stretching and contracting in rapid waves; and the deer, high, arching over the ground, propelled by legs like springy levers. Within seconds, Luke is swallowed by the darkness and only the deers' white tails can be seen, bobbing like wood sprites among the trees.

The night makes us stealthy. When the police car's long beams swing in at the entrance, I become an outlaw. Luke and I scoot back by the steeplechase ring and I watch—one leg up on the railing—with the smug omniscience of one who can see but can't be seen. The car has a spotlight that scans to the side, making it look like one of those deep-sea submersibles that light up the dark ocean bottom. I try to wear dark clothing, but if I have on light things, I line up my body with one of the six-foot fence posts to camouflage myself.

Last winter, I came upon a new set of animal tracks after a freshly fallen snow. They weren't the tracks of rabbits or raccoons. They looked like the tracks of a dog, but a solitary one with a very narrow foot.

I studied it very closely, because there had been a fox sighting only a week before. A man doing his morning walk had seen one loping along the railroad tracks. He posted the news on the town's Web site. I was envious. I hadn't seen a fox since the one I saw stalking the woodchuck many years ago.

I followed the tracks, a neat dotted line with no hesitations or meandering, the track of an animal with a purpose and a destination. As I followed, I understood how Native Americans came to identify with the animals they hunted. When you follow another creature's tracks, you step on the same ground, see what it saw, and begin to intuit its motives. Pretty soon, you're inside its skin.

At our end of the long road, it veered in the direction of the stables. It went under the fence of a corral and headed straight for the big barn. Luke and I stopped there. Looking through my fox eyes, I saw food in that barn—mice, horse feed, what have you. That made sense. Why knock yourself out in a snow-covered landscape when there was a nice barn available?

Winter turned into spring and I still hadn't seen a fox. Then in June, I began to hear strange sounds. Were they squawks? Screeches? No, more like raspy coughs. It was a little unnerving. And it was coming from all over—by the railroad tracks, the steeplechase ring, the perimeter of the stables.

Finally, I brought a flashlight. It was a moonless night and the fireflies were flashing like electrical sparks. The corridor alongside the steeplechase ring was so thick with them it looked like the path to Neverland. I heard something panting and jingling near me in the darkness. I started, then saw it was Jester. Immediately, the two dogs ran off together. I watched as they darted among the hurdles of a practice ring. That's how it is with dogs, sometimes. You think you're on a serious quest and they get silly on you.

I leaned on the top fence rail and clicked on my flashlight. A fifty-yard-long tube of light shot out. I cast it across the steeplechase ring. It was like fishing. Pretty soon, I had one. Two yellow lights shone back at me. For a second, I thought they were fireflies, but the lights glowed steadily instead of winking.

Something Joe the hunter once said popped into my head. He was talking about a wolf-dog hybrid he once had, and I had asked him how he was so sure it was half wolf.

"From the eyes," he said. "A dog's eyes glow red, a wolf's eyes glow yellow."

Then the animal turned, and just before it disappeared behind the jumping obstacle, I saw its bushy tail.

Fox.

Those strange squawks and raspy coughs had been its bark.

Over the next several nights, I saw more pairs of eyes. One night pulling up in the car at the end of the dead-end street, my headlights picked up two young ones walking light as kittens down the center of the railroad tracks.

A family of foxes! Maybe more.

I went to the Internet. The fox's preferred habitat, I learned, was between wild and settled land, a perfect description of this place. There was all sorts of fascinating lore. Their reputation for cleverness, for example, was well earned. Foxes did a trick called "charming," in which they distracted their prey with acrobatics, somersaults and tail chasing, until the fascinated bird or rabbit lost all sense of danger. Then the fox pounced. What other animal had such tricks? A surprising number of legends and stories had foxes turning into people or casting off their human disguise to reveal that they'd been foxes all along.

My town felt like a different place with this shape-shifting trickster living among us.

One night, I shined my flashlight in the direction of the sloped jumping obstacle and picked up the now-familiar eyes. The fox was sitting on the flat top of the ramp. It reminded me of Egyptian carvings of Anubis, the jackal-like god of the afterlife who was sometimes depicted sitting on a throne-like pedestal. It was remarkable how much the fox's posture and attitude resembled that statue, as if it were declaring its preeminence here.

And why not? It was the omnivore at the apex of the Meadowlands' food chain. There was hardly an edible thing this land produced that didn't pass through its gullet: berries, buds, fruit, grasshoppers, birds, turtle eggs, frogs, mice, rabbits, snakes, muskrats, woodchucks. North and I saw evidence of this after we learned to identify its scat, which it boldly deposited at every Meadowlands' trail fork and intersection. We even found it on our plank across the canal. We came upon signs of kills—heaps of blue jay and mockingbird feathers and the remains of a good-size gosling. The fur of its mammal prey passed out of the fox's body twirled into spirals and, after all else had decomposed, lay bleached on the trail like someone's clipped-off pigtail.

The fox ate everything but nothing ate it.

One evening, around twilight, I surprised one in an empty corral. Luke squeezed himself under the fence and was after it, but the fox was far too clever and agile to be caught by a dog. It ran the length of nine or ten corrals, jumping between the narrowly spaced rails—rather, *flowing* between the rails, demonstrating where those legends about shape-shifting came from.

Those luminous yellow eyes seemed to shine across the gulf between the wild world and the tame one. Here was the very spirit of wildness, wilder—if you were to believe the stories—than even the other wild animals, a kind of outlaw creature that literally ran circles around the rest of them. Despite its catlike eyes and that extravagant, almost feline tail, it was a member of the canine family like the jackal, the wolf, the coyote, and . . . my Luke.

If all that weren't enough to make someone wonder if Providence might have a message for him, this wild canid that had suddenly seemed to take possession of our Meadowlands had a reputation for being magical. It was the focus of countless legends and stories, from Europe's trickster Reynard to China's shape-changing Huli jing to Japan's wise and magical kitsune to Korea's demoniacal kumiho. They could fly or make themselves invisible. They could be spirits, ghosts, or naughty poltergeist. They could turn themselves into almost any shape—a tree, a moon, or a fog. Mostly, however, they turned into people—or the people turned into foxes.

Sometimes, looking into those luminous eyes, I had the eerie sensation that I was seeing myself. Or my future self. With my imagination filled to the brim with these fantastic legends, I felt only one step away from foxhood. Was this where my journey had been leading me? Had these paths I followed through woods and meadow and marshland been leading me to the brink of some metamorphosis? Wasn't I already acting like a fox? Didn't I prefer this edge between the wild and the settled? Didn't I dart around in the darkness eluding the police? I could see it all coming. I had only to surrender to my yearnings, give up my upright life, and, with a raspy bark, run off on all fours, pursued by my ecstatic dog!

Dog Walks Man

EPILOGUE

North called the other day. "I need a dog walk," he said, like a man at the end of his rope. He'd been through a crisis and wanted the therapeutic benefits of a walk through the Meadowlands with a friend and his dog.

How often do friends call with troubles and you wonder if, really, there is anything you can say that would help? But I didn't feel that way. I put Luke in the car and drove over to North's house, confident that I had something to offer—or that Luke did. I wouldn't have felt so sure on my own.

Why? What does a dog bring to the experience of going out into the world that makes it so much better than going out by yourself or with another person?

Very simply, dogs connect you to nature. They bring the same powerful animal certainty to the natural world that they bring to the human family. *This is where we come from*, dogs remind us, the ever-forgetful ones. *These places are special. The woods. The grassy field. The riverbank. The jungly wild.*

I remember once letting Pete loose in the park and thinking: *a dog in a meadow doesn't know how to be unhappy.* A dog's headlong engagement with the world, its trust that nature will receive it with open arms, is something few of us can muster on our own. We need a little help from a friend with two feet in each world.

Thoreau's Walden, now a state park, may be lost to us as a wild place. And few modern people could move there even if it were magically restored to its 1845 state. But we still have dogs, and dogs can usually be counted on to find that surviving scrap of wildness out on the fringe, which, really, was all that Thoreau had or needed—a bit of wild fringe amid railroads, villages, and farms. The dog is a four-legged Walden. It points us in the right direction and brings us back to the same place again and again until, like children in front of a diorama, we finally learn to see.

When Claire was in high school, she did some community service at the county hospital. She had Pete certified as a "therapy dog," and the two of them went around to visit patients. They were a big hit and I can understand why. If I am ever languishing in a public institution, penniless and infirm, I can't imagine a sweeter elixir than the arrival of someone like my daughter—kind, bright, fair of face—leading a big, friendly poodle who wants nothing more than to be scratched around the ears.

I recalled this service of theirs when, a few years later, Claire was home from college and getting through a rough patch in life. Perhaps a little "dog-walking therapy," I suggested, only half-jokingly, as I stood at the front door with Luke and Pete, both of them literally vibrating in anticipation of the morning walk.

She considered, seemed about to decline, then, in the spirit of humoring me, said "Oh, why not?"

It was February, in the middle of a snowy winter. It snowed early and the snow stayed on the ground, barely melting before another storm added to it. Bundled up in boots, scarves, ski caps, gloves, and parkas, we felt like an adventure awaited us. The dogs were at their shaggiest, unbothered by the cold and in love with the snow. Pete was getting a little creaky, it was true, but was still up for anything. He put his front legs on the tailgate, and Claire boosted him into the back. And then we were off, the four of us, on our way to the Outpost.

We had no heart-to-heart talks that day. This wasn't about that. This was about getting outside and offering up the knot of the infernal self to nature.

Luke poked at the frozen puddles with his paws, confused as to what mischief had suddenly turned water hard. Down at the Water Hole's edge, he stepped out onto the solid greenish surface in a defensive crouch and took a few slow-motion steps, looking like a slinky cartoon dog.

We didn't see North that week, but Joe was around. The veteran hunter, made aware of Claire's feelings about animals, kept his lips zipped about deer and snow-goose hunting and woodchuck recipes. They looked as different as two people could: Claire, willowy with a profile like a Victorian cameo; and Joe, barrel-chested, with a face like a bag of walnuts. As red as that face got from the cold, I could still see him blush a little in Claire's presence.

Our animal friend that winter was a great blue heron, a prehistoric looking bird that had come down from some northern latitude to winter in the Meadowlands. No matter how cold it was, this heron found a small spot of open, moving water in which to fish. It fished in the classic crane style, standing stock-still on one leg, ready to jab its beak down into the water.

It always cheered me to see it there, because its presence contradicted what people commonly believed about these waters—that they were polluted and incapable of supporting life. The heron's continued presence here—and it came back year after year, sometimes in the company of another—said these waters had enough fish to support such a large predator.

It was impossible to sneak up on. It was so still and so focused on any sound or movement that it detected us long before we detected it. We'd be walking along, the dogs out in front, and there it would be, already above the tops of the reeds, rising silently, slowly, like an airborne scarecrow. Given all the effort it took for it to get aloft, you'd have expected it to be angry at our interruptions. But unlike the geese or the crows that scolded or complained, this passive and doleful bird departed in stoical silence. Once it gained altitude, it tucked its legs up, curled its long neck back on itself, and, with its broad wingspan and long, pointed beak, assumed the appearance of a pterodactyl.

When I see it in my mind's eye today, I realize how much it symbolized the problem at hand, that struggle with mood that everyone confronts at one time or another in life. Every day, we saw it defy gravity and somehow get up in the sky.

There were tracks everywhere that winter—the meandering grooves in the snow left by tunneling mice, the quick-hop tracks of rabbits, and, of course, those from all our own trampings to and fro. There were tracks everywhere except in the meadow, where no one had ventured. This gave us an idea. While I restrained the dogs, Claire laid a line of tracks about fifteen yards out into this pristine white slate. Then she very carefully walked backward, placing each foot neatly into its own print. When she finished, a line of footprints went out into the snowy meadow and abruptly stopped, as if a person had walked out there, paused, and taken flight.

Pete was still a leggy puppy and I was still a stranger to our storybook neighborhood when our dog-walking odyssey began. We hadn't yet progressed much past the blocks around our house. One balmy night we headed up the hill. It was about ten o'clock, late enough that the streets were empty, but early enough that lights were on in all the houses. Pete was still on the leash back then, and had so much excess energy that I could let him pull me a bit up the hill, a not-unpleasant sensation.

Pete looked back over his shoulder, throwing me one of those doggy smiles that assured me something out of the ordinary was going to happen. This time, he was right. The night had a magical feel. We walked beneath those great trees, trunks shooting up eighty, ninety, a hundred feet, trees that shrunk adults to the size of Hansel and Gretel.

Between the branches, a crescent moon swayed as bold as a theater prop on its nail. Then, out of the darkness came a voice. A girl was singing somewhere. She was at an upstairs window, lost among the treetops. This was spring and nature was pressing and pushing in every direction. It had cranked up its great machine and was infusing life into seeds, buds, and cocoons. Leaves were unfolding. Blossoms lured pollen-spreading insects into their voluptuous interiors. Tiny tree frogs chirped. Beneath the leaf mold, ladybugs stirred. This girl's song was part of that push, that chorus, that coming-to-life. She sang in a beguiling languid voice that would suddenly swell with longing. I couldn't see her, didn't need to see her. She was a reminder that we are part of nature, too. She was our human voice in the spring chorus.

It was the first of many gifts.

I couldn't possibly know all that lay ahead as I followed my frisky guide up the hill that night. Pete's repeated lesson to me was that I had to stay alive to possibilities, which I'm still trying to do. At times, I've lost the knack for it, and gone for days like a sleep-walker, unable to remember what I ever found so interesting. Then something shifts. A chink opens up in the world's armor. And I'm in business again.

ACKNOWLEDGMENTS

I would like to thank my agent, Laurie Abkemeier, whose encouragement, insight, and keen editing skills helped shape the manuscript. I also want to thank my editor Holly Rubino, who saw everything I was trying to do and helped sharpen the writing to that end. Thanks also to the other people at Globe Pequot: Janice Goldklang, Diana Nuhn, and Greg Hyman. I owe a great deal to my friend North Peterson for his companionship, wisdom, and unfaltering faith in this project over countless miles of dog walking. I thank the people who read and commented on the manuscript: Bob Pillitteri, Mark Schwerin, Joey Schwerin, Jackie Peterson, Ann Thurlow, Jim Wright, Jean Arbeiter, Barbara Hoffman, Garby Leon, Shannon Mow, and Anthony Santuoso. Thanks also to Gil Hawkins of the Overpeck Preserve for his stewardship of our town's precious bit of the wild. I am deeply grateful for the patience and support of my wife, Janet, and to our children, Claire and Alex, who needed no persuading that an ordinary dog walk could be a special thing.

John Zeaman is a freelance art critic and the author of several books for children, including *How the Wolf Became the Dog*. He has won numerous awards for his work and was three times honored by the Manhattan-based Society of Silurians, the nation's oldest press club, for his newspaper column on design in the everyday world. He lives in Leonia, New Jersey, with his wife, Janet Chatfield. They have two grown children.